Digital Media and Society Series

New technologies are fundamentally altering the ways in which I communicate. This series from Polity aims to provide a set of books that make available for a broad readership cutting-edge research and thinking on digital media and their social contexts. Taken as a whole, the series will examine questions about the impact of network technology and digital media on society in all its facets, including economics, culture and politics.

Published:

Jean Burgess and Joshua Green, *YouTube*
Mark Deuze, *Media Work*
Charles Ess, *Digital Media Ethics*
Alexander Halavais, *Search Engine Society*
Robert Hassan, *The Information Society*
Tim Jordan, *Hacking*
Rich Ling and Jonathan Donner, *Mobile Communication*
Donald Matheson and Stuart Allan, *Digital War Reporting*
Jill Walker Rettberg, *Blogging*
Patrik Wikström, *The Music Industry*

The right of Patrik Wikström to be identified as Author of this Work has been asserted in accordance with the UK Copyright, Designs and Patents Act 1988.

First published in 2009 by Polity Press

Polity Press
65 Bridge Street
Cambridge CB2 1UR, UK

Polity Press
350 Main Street
Malden, MA 02148, USA

ISBN-13: 978-0-7456-4389-2
ISBN-13: 978-0-7456-4390-8 (pb)

A catalogue record for this book is available from the British Library.

Typeset in 10.25 on 13 pt FF Scala
by Servis Filmsetting Ltd, Stockport, Cheshire
Printed and bound by MPG Books Group, Bodmin, UK

The publisher has used its best endeavours to ensure that the URLs for external websites referred to in this book are correct and active at the time of going to press. However, the publisher has no responsibility for the websites and can make no guarantee that a site will remain live or that the content is or will remain appropriate.

Every effort has been made to trace all copyright holders, but if any have been inadvertently overlooked the publishers will be pleased to include any necessary credits in any subsequent reprint or edition.

For further information on Polity, visit our website: www.politybooks.com

The Music Industry: Music in the Cloud

PATRIK WIKSTRÖM

polity

For Pia

Contents

List of Figures and Tables   viii
Acknowledgments   x

Introduction – Music in the Cloud   1

1   A Copyright Industry   12

2   Inside the Music Industry   46

3   Music and the Media   85

4   Making Music   118

5   The Social and Creative Music Fan   147

6   Future Sounds   170

Notes   179
References   183
Index   198

List of Figures and Tables

Figure 0.1	Cloud as an Internet metaphor	3
Figure 0.2	Increased connectivity causes the music firms to lose their ability to control the flow of information	6
Figure 2.1	Musical networks	50
Figure 2.2	Production/consumption systems of popular music	52
Figure 2.3	The organization of the recording industry	54
Figure 2.4	A music publishing industry value chain	58
Figure 2.5	Global music sales by format	65
Figure 2.6	Milestones in music technology development	66
Figure 2.7	Recorded music sales 2008	70
Figure 2.8	Noteworthy mergers and acquisitions during the development of Universal Music Group	74
Figure 2.9	Noteworthy mergers and acquisitions during the development of Sony Music	76
Figure 2.10	Noteworthy mergers and acquisitions during the development of Warner Music Group	79
Figure 2.11	Noteworthy mergers and acquisitions during the development of EMI Group	81
Figure 3.1	The audience–media engine	86
Figure 3.2	Increase of licensing revenues 1995–2008	94
Figure 5.1	Continuing growth in numbers of simultaneous P2P users worldwide	154

Table 1.1   Levels of aggregation and the facets of the
             production of culture perspective   44
Table 2.1   The music industry as defined by the
             British government   48
Table 2.2   The music industry according to Engström
             and Hallencreutz   48
Table 2.3   The domestic music share of the world's
             forty-two largest music markets   72
Table 4.1   The average age of top-10 global superstars 131

Acknowledgments

First I would like to thank all the informants whom I have interviewed during the years. Your thoughts are at the centre of this work and, without your involvement, the project would not have been conceivable. I would also like to send a thank you to everyone else in the academia and the industry whom I have been fortunate enough to meet: thank you for helping me shape this book by giving me inspiration, encouragement and criticism along the way. Lastly, I would like to thank Andrea Drugan and her team at Polity Press who have been there for me through the ups and the downs of the project.

Introduction – Music in the Cloud

A Sunday in early March 2008, the Industrial rock megastar Trent Reznor, a.k.a. Nine Inch Nails, released his seventh studio project, *Ghosts I–IV*. The project consists in total of thirty-six instrumental songs recorded during ten weeks in the autumn of 2007. Even though Nine Inch Nails is a global brand and Trent Reznor has millions of devoted fans all over the world, he was at the time without a contract with a major record label after having ended a relationship with the Universal label, Interscope Records. 'As of right now Nine Inch Nails is a totally free agent, free of any recording contract with any label', Reznor wrote on the band's website, 'I have been under recording contracts for 18 years and have watched the business radically mutate from one thing to something inherently very different and it gives me great pleasure to be able to finally have a direct relationship with the audience as I see fit and appropriate.' For *Ghosts I–IV*, Reznor decided that the appropriate distribution channel would be the official Nine Inch Nails website 'nin.com'. He also chose to release the songs under a licence which allowed fans to remix and redistribute the work in a multitude of different formats (cf. p. 177). On 13 March, Reznor launched the second phase of the project. First, multitrack versions of a number of songs from *Ghosts* were added to the remix section of 'nin.com' where fans could upload their own remixes, listen to and review the remixes from other fans, vote for their favourites, and so on. Second, Reznor launched an Internet-based 'Film Festival' on YouTube where he invited fans to create and upload their visual interpretations of the songs.

The fans' reception of the *Ghosts* project cannot be labelled as anything but exceptional.

At the end of 2008 fans had uploaded over 2000 videos to the Film Festival, and an unknown but large number of user-generated remixes had been posted to 'remix.nin.com'. Besides remixing and uploading the tracks from *Ghosts I–IV*, fans were also able to download nine of the original songs for free from the website. They were also offered four other product packages ranging from a '$5 Download' which included all thirty-six songs in various formats to a '$300 Ultra Deluxe Limited Edition Package' which included downloads, CDs, DVDs and glossy booklets, all signed by Reznor himself. According to Reznor, during the first week after the launch 781,917 transactions generated $1,619,420 in sales revenue. In addition, the '$5 Download' version was released on Amazon MP3 Downloads and remained as one of their top-selling albums at least during March and April 2008.[1] It is notable that this result was achieved while the album, in its entirety, obviously also was available via various illegal file-sharing networks and services.

Even though Reznor's *Ghosts I–IV* is a rather unusual case, it beautifully encapsulates the music industry a decade after Shawn Fanning[2] released Napster and peer-to-peer file-sharing to the masses and changed the music industry forever. Certainly, various digital technologies were used to create, promote and distribute *Ghosts I–IV*, but what makes the project even more significant is how these technologies shaped its fundamental structure and logic. The *Ghosts I–IV* project has evolved pretty far from the twentieth century when vertically integrated multinational music companies could control how, when and where their albums were released, promoted and distributed. The core of the project is not the thirty-six tracks recorded in Reznor's recording studio in the outskirts of Beverly Hills. Rather it is Reznor's relationship with his fans and in the thousands of remixes, videos, comments and blog posts uploaded to nin.com, YouTube, ninremixes.com and a host of other more or less shady places in the Cloud.

'The Cloud' has been used as a metaphor to denote the Internet since the late 1960s and early 1970s when Vinton Cerf, Robert

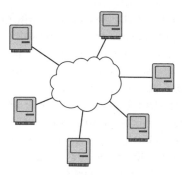

Figure 0.1 Cloud as an Internet metaphor

Kahn, Robert Metcalfe, Leonard Kleinrock, Larry Roberts and many others invented the technologies behind the network of networks. A cloud was considered to be a useful and vague enough symbol which could be used to summarize all the resources, cables and gadgets which connected the computers at the nodes of the network (Figure 0.1). These days, 'The Cloud' still is used as a metaphor for the Internet, but it also conveys other meanings. For more than twenty years, the computer manufacturer Sun Microsystems has pushed the slogan 'The Network is the Computer'. Sun suggested back in those days that the resources in the Cloud soon would become so powerful that the computers at the network nodes no longer had to be sophisticated and expensive but could be made extremely simple and cheap. Eventually, technology did not choose exactly that path, but, in some respects, what during recent years has been promoted as 'Web 2.0' to a large extent is based on the basic principles suggested by Sun. Web 2.0 is usually a term used to denote a family of Web-based services which are far more complex than the traditional, relatively static information-based Web pages. Web 2.0 services are really full-fledged Web-based software which enable users to socialize with friends and family, store and edit photos, listen to and remix music and many other things. For instance, in the area of productivity software, Web 2.0 services make it possible for users to subscribe to word-processing, spreadsheets, email, calendars and similar resources, rather than to purchase the traditional Office package from Microsoft (e.g. Carr 2008).

In this book, I apply the concept of '. . . in the Cloud' to the field of music to emphasize how the music industry during less than a decade has completely shifted its centre of gravity from the physical to the virtual – from the Disk to the Cloud. Many years have passed since the young music audience used to play a CD during a party, but today it is also less common that they play MP3s stored on their computers or iPods. Increasingly, they listen to music from YouTube, last.fm, Lala, Spotify, remix.nin. com, or some other Web-based music service; or they download a decent party mix from a file-sharing network such as BitComet or LimeWire. Music is no longer something the mainstream audience owns and collects – Music is in the Cloud.

The purpose of this book is to explore the transformation of the music industry which is manifested by projects such as *Ghosts I–IV*. Of course, it is not the first time the music industry has been transformed by changes in the media environment. Changes in broadcast radio programming during the 1950s, the compact cassette during the 1970s and the deregulation of media ownership during the 1990s all had tremendous impact on the structure and logic of the industry. However, I believe the transformation which took place during the first decade of the twenty-first century is even more dramatic than the previous ones. Certainly, as I will stress in this book, there are many aspects of the old music industry which remain the same, regardless of whether the music is on the Disk or in the Cloud. However, the transformation is of such a magnitude that it is relevant to talk about a 'new' music industry dynamics or a 'new music economy', as it sometimes has been referred to (D'Arcangelo 2007; Denis 2008; Goodman 2008). During a seminar in May 2008, Corey Denis tried to define the 'new music economy' by listing a number of specific components which the seminar participants deemed as necessary to make the new music economy tick.[3] Their conclusions are definitely interesting but I choose to cut the cake somewhat differently and argue that there are three basic features which characterize the new music industry dynamics.

Connectivity vs. control

In order to make a living in the old music economy it was all about *control* – a music firm's top priority was to maximize the revenues from each individual piece of intellectual property and to minimize unauthorized use. In the new music economy, it is still important to *know* how one's intellectual property is used by the audience but it is more or less impossible to regulate and police that use. I borrow a term from network theory – connectivity – to explain the new situation. Connectivity is a measure of how well the members of a network are connected. A network is considered to have a *high* level of connectivity if most of its members are connected to each other, and vice versa. In figure 0.2, the network to the left has lower connectivity than the network to the right. In a network with high connectivity, information, money, fads, norms etc., easily flow between the members (e.g. Watts 2003).

In the old music economy, the network constituted by music companies and the audience had a relatively low level of connectivity. Basically, there were strong connections from the music firms to the audience, but only weak connections between the members of the audience (illustrated by the left network in figure 0.2). Consequently, the flow of music could relatively easily be controlled by the music firms since it was unable to flow between separated parts of the audience.

In the new music economy, the importance of physical music distribution and mass media has been radically reduced, while the importance of Internet media has exploded. These new communication technologies have an entirely different structure from the previous hierarchical media. The technologies lower the barriers which previously have restricted the capability to distribute information to the network, i.e. the capability to upload information to the Cloud. Now, the capability to upload is theoretically accessible to everyone connected to the network.

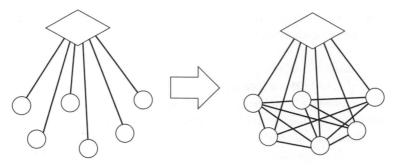

Figure 0.2 Increased connectivity causes the music firms to lose their ability to control the flow of information

As a consequence, the connectivity of the 'audience–music firm' network has increased, which in turn has caused the music firms to lose their ability to control the flow of information. In a nutshell, the new music industry dynamics is characterized by high connectivity and little control.

Service vs. product
In the old music economy, the content (music) and the medium (disk) were inseparable, and the music industry clearly was an industry of physical goods. In the new music economy, characterized by high connectivity and little control, it becomes increasingly difficult to charge a premium for discrete chunks of information. As soon as some kind of information is uploaded to the Cloud, it is instantly universally accessible to everyone connected to the Cloud. In such a 'friction-free network',[4] the commercial *value of providing access* to an individual track is infinitesimally close to zero. However, it should immediately be noted that I do not claim that the *value of a song* is zero or even close to zero. It has been argued that 'in the future', music will be like water or electricity (e.g. Kusek & Leonard 2005). I strongly object to both water and electricity as metaphors of music. Music is an art form – it is not water. Great art which moves people is created by unique individuals with exceptional talents and is definitely not chargeable by the minute or the megabyte.

But there are other things which remain chargeable. In a world where information is abundant, people may not be willing to pay a premium for basic access to that information, but they are most likely willing to pay for services which help them navigate through the vast amounts of information. If music is thought of as a *service* it is possible to fathom consumer propositions which are both valuable to the audience and respectful to the work of the creative artists. More on that later in this book.

Amateur vs. professional
The role of the creative artist is the most respected and admired in the music industrial ecosystem. Nine Inch Nails, Regina Spector, Stevie Wonder, Celine Dion are all powerful brands which appeal to millions of fans all over the world. I praise these extraordinarily talented individuals and recognize their work as the music industry's centre of gravity. However, in the new music economy, the relationship between these brands, their art and the audience is changed. The increased connectivity of the audience network combined with various kinds of music production tools enable 'non-professionals' to create, remix and publish content online. This does not necessarily imply that, in the new music economy, *every* music listener also is an amateur musician, but nevertheless a considerable share of the audience do create and upload content to the Cloud. For instance, research into the world of fan fiction shows that approximately 5 per cent of a user population creates and uploads content, 12 per cent comments on that content and 24 per cent actively reads the content and the comments (Olin-Scheller & Wikström 2009). Bradley Horowitz, VP at Google and formerly VP at Yahoo!, reports similar results from studies of user behaviour at Yahoo! Groups (Horowitz 2006). It is not entirely unrealistic to assume that those fans who create, remix and upload content also are the most dedicated and loyal. It is also quite likely that they are the ones who spend the most on concerts, merchandise etc. Based on those two assumptions, it makes sense for music firms to secure a good relationship with this part of the audience,

encourage their creative desires and do their best not to push them away.

To sum up: the new music industry dynamics is character-ized by high connectivity and little control; music provided as a service; and increased amateur creativity. The driver of all these changes is primarily the development of digital information and communication technologies. The music industry started its journey into the 'digital age' a long time ago, during the 1970s, when digital technologies were introduced in the areas of music production and recording. During the 1980s, primarily due to the introduction of the compact disk, the use of these technolo-gies expanded to music distribution. Lastly, during the late 1990s and early 2000s, Internet technologies were the most important drivers of change, and ultimately brought every remaining part of the music business, including promotion and talent develop-ment, into the realm of digital technology.

The number of technological innovations related to this third period of change has literally exploded: BitTorrent, Facebook, iMeem, iTunes/iPod, Lala, Last.fm, LimeWire, MySpace, Napster, Pandora, Qtrax, Rhapsody, SpiralFrog, Spotify, are only a few out of an overwhelming amount of music technology brands. Although many of these innovations may be relevant as markers of the new music industry dynamics, this study will not analyse the details of any such specific innovation. My ambition is rather to stay above the level of these 'technological ripples' and try to discern the long-term patterns which are created by the innovations in aggregate.

During this period of change I have been able to meet a large number of music industry professionals to discuss their understanding of the new dynamics. I use quotes from these interviews to illustrate and strengthen the reasoning. In order to ensure the anonymity of the informants I conceal their iden-tities in relation to their quotes and introduce them by their profession – for example 'product manager' or 'producer'. I conducted interviews with professionals from Sweden, the UK and the US. Why these countries, one might ask? The UK and the US warrant the attention of our study since they are two of the largest and most influential national music markets in the world (IFPI 2007), in terms of both consumption and production. Sweden is a much smaller market than the other two, but a nation with a 'fantastically rich music culture' (BBC News 2006) and a history as a strong exporter of popular music (e.g, ExMS 2005). Sweden is also interesting since it is a country with an advanced information technology infrastructure and a copyright legislation which has been slow to adapt to international treaties (e.g. Keller 2006). This combination has nurtured an environment which once established Sweden as 'a haven for copyright infringement' (BBC News 2006; Reuters 2006).

The study does not try to explain any *differences* between the behaviour of the three markets. Rather, the study focuses on the *similarities* between the three. When certain behaviour is occurring in all three markets, it is assumed to be indicating that the dynamics is of significance and should be included in the overall reasoning. The term 'the music industry' is often used in the text, and formally it is a reference to the national music industries in the three countries included in the study. However, the music industry is one of the copyright industries where national borders are only of minor significance. Most markets are dominated by a handful o fmultinational organizations, and, thus, innovations, practices, people and routines easily flow across national borders. It may consequently be possible to extend the validity of the findings presented by this srudy beyond the three countries. At least the European Union and North America could be included, and perhaps also the other members of the OECD. Finally it should be noted that the three markets are examined on a national level only and no attention is paid to the dynamics of local markets within each territory.

The structure of the book

This is a book about the Cloud-based music industry. I argue that this industry is characterized by high connectivity and little control; music provided as a service; and increased amateur creativity.

In chapter 1 I start out by labelling the music industry as a 'copyright industry'. I discuss characteristics and features which distinguish these industries from other, 'non-copyright industries'. I then pay attention to the debate about the possible tension between profit maximization and creativity. Lastly, I present my theoretical platform which is based on frameworks from organizational theory, social learning theory and the sociology of culture.

In the second chapter I turn the attention to the inside of the music industry. I believe that it is important to understand the workings of the traditional music industry in order to recognize the significance of the change that has created the new music industry dynamics. I therefore use well-established music industry models to explain and discuss the music industry and its three sub-sectors; recorded music, music publishing and live music. I give an account of the history of the industry and present some basic facts related to the six largest multinational industry players (Universal Music Group, Sony Music Entertainment, Warner Music Group, EMI Group, Sony/ATV Music Publishing and Live Nation).

After having introduced and contextualized the music industry I use the next three chapters to analyse different aspects of the transformation of the industry.

In chapter 3 I analyse the relationship between recorded music, media and audiences. I start out by presenting a model of this relationship used to support an analysis of the changes in the media environment. I focus on how the increased connectivity of the audience–music firm network shapes the new music economy and I introduce concepts such as 'audience fragmentation' and 'option value blurring'. The analysis is particularly focused on the recorded music sector and the music licensing sector. In the area of music licensing, I examine the changing roles of music publishing and the music publisher in the new music industry dynamics. In the area of the recorded music sector, I focus on a range of new business models which have been developed by music business entrepreneurs. I examine the models' viability in the light of the shifting levels of connectivity and control and discuss the concept of music as a service.

Chapter 4 is focused on music making. I have previously noted that one of the most important characteristics of the new music economy is the rise of amateur creativity and the increase of so-called user-generated content. However, in this chapter I will focus on the *professional* making of music, both in the studio and on stage. I explore the changes in the production system of popular music, primarily related to the roles and careers of songwriters, artists and producers, and to the changes in the institutions and structures of that system.

In chapter 5 I focus on the role of music fans, and how this affects every aspect of the new music economy, including distribution, promotion, production and talent development. I examine how fans' desire to listen to music, use music and express themselves through music sometimes is in conflict with copyright legislation.

Finally I take the discussion into the future and reflect on how the trends of today will shape the music industry of tomorrow.

1

A Copyright Industry

In this chapter I argue that the contemporary music industry is best understood as a 'copyright industry'. I explain why this is an important starting point in the digital age and argue for the necessity of this shift in perspective. I then develop a theoretical platform based on my borrowing of frameworks from organizational theory, social learning theory and the sociology of culture.

Defining industries

Most scholars, regardless of discipline, try to classify and label the objects they research. Music industry scholars do not deviate from this norm and during the development of the field the music industry has been categorized as a 'creative industry', an 'experience industry' or a 'cultural industry', to name but a few. In this section I examine some of these labels, and I also argue why I prefer to use the term 'copyright industry'.

The oldest label, the 'culture industry', is usually traced back to the Frankfurt School of Critical Theory and its most recognized scholars Max Horkheimer and Theodor Adorno. Between 1935 and 1949 the research institute was relocated to Columbia University in New York, and it was during this period that Horkheimer and Adorno wrote their most important work,[5] the *Dialektik der Aufklärung* (1944). In this very influential and pessimistic book, Horkheimer and Adorno outline how the world is moving closer to self-destruction. One of the chapters of the book examines the 'culture industry', where they argue that the culture industry is the result of a process where an increase in media and communication technologies leads to the *industrial* production,

circulation and consumption of cultural *commodities*. The indus-
trialization of these processes results in formulaic, standardized,
repetitive, pre-digested products which reduce the audience to a
'child-like' state. (e.g. Adorno 1941; Horkheimer & Adorno 1944;
Hesmondhalgh 2002; Negus 1996 & 1997).

During the 1970s, French scholars (e.g. Miège 1979) and
policy-makers (e.g. Girard 1981) decided to pick up the term.
However, they also decided to revise its meaning considerably. First, they changed its form from singular to plural
(cultural industries) to denote the diversity between different
cultural industries. Second, they rejected the pessimistic and
nostalgic position assumed by the Frankfurt School. Instead
they argued that the commodification of culture, facilitated by
new technologies, also had its positive sides. For instance the
new technologies enabled innovation, and, in addition, ordinary
people were allowed access to culture that previously had been
out of their reach. Third, while Horkheimer and Adorno considered the field of popular, industrialized culture as frozen and
static, these scholars argued that the cultural industries represent a dynamic zone of continuing struggle between commerce
and art (Hesmondhalgh 2002:15–17; Towse 2001:25).

The early definitions of cultural industries and cultural products are not radically different from today. Hirsch defined
cultural products as 'nonmaterial goods directed at a public of
consumers, for whom they generally serve an aesthetic or expressive, rather than utilitarian function' (1972:641) Three decades
later, the definitions suggested by scholars such as Throsby
(2001) and Hesmondhalgh (2002) are very similar to Hirsch's
explanation. Hesmondhalgh, for instance, considers the cultural
industries as 'industries based upon the industrial production
and circulation of texts, and which are centrally reliant on the
work of symbol creators' (2002:14).

Hesmondhalgh's definition requires two comments. First, the
interpretation of the term 'text'. All cultural artefacts could be considered as texts. However, some cultural artefacts can be mainly
functional (e.g. cars, clothes, furniture) while other artefacts are

mainly communicative (e.g. songs, images, stories, perform-ances). In his definition of cultural industries, Hesmondhalgh is only referring to the latter, that is to say texts that are mainly communicative or symbolic in their nature (2002:12). Second, instead of using the term 'artist', Hesmondhalgh uses the term 'symbol creators' for those who make up, interpret or rework these texts (2002:4–5).

When explicitly defining which industries are cultural and which are not, Girard suggested that broadcasting, pub-lishing, music and film should be included (Girard 1981). Hesmondhalgh's list of 'core cultural industries' is similar to Girard's, but with the addition of advertising and interactive media[6] (Hesmondhalgh 2002:12). Girard did actually consider Advertising as one of the cultural industries, and it is quite understandable why in 1981 he did not choose to add interactive media to the list.

The term 'cultural industries' is a rather appealing label with several strengths. The term has a long heritage and has been widely accepted by scholars. However, the term has also been criticized. For instance, Cunningham (2005) argues that 'cul-tural industries' is an outdated term that is linked to analogue media, nationalistic cultural policies, neoclassical economics applied to the arts etc. Several other alternative terms aimed at defining the same industries (including the music industry) have therefore been suggested. In policy circles, terms such as 'crea-tive industries' and 'experience industries' have become very popular. These definitions usually have a wider scope than the original term and include industries or activities such as archi-tecture, design, fashion, performing arts, crafts and sometimes even tourism, sport and restaurants.

These newer concepts have radically changed the relationship between government and culture. As Hartley describes it:

> The 'creative industries' idea brought creativity from the back door of government, where it had sat for decades holding out the tin cup for arts subsidy [. . .] to the front door, where it was introduced to the wealth-creating portfolios, the emergent

industry departments, and the enterprise support programs. [. . .] Creative industries [helped] revitalize cities and regions that had moved out of heavy industry, had never developed a strong manufacturing base or who were over-exposed to declining IT industries. (Hartley 2005: 19)

Manchester, UK, and Hultsfred, Sweden, are but two examples of many such governmental reform initiatives (Bjälesjö 2005; O'Connor 2000). This focus on regional development has also led to an increased interest in these industries by economic geography scholars (e.g. Hallencreutz 2002; Leyshon 2001; Power 2003). In addition, the mapping of these industries has turned into a lucrative business for scholars and consultants alike. Many regions and nations decide they need healthy creative industries and, in order to achieve that goal, the definition of what is actually a part of these industries differs from nation to nation and region to region.

For instance, in Sweden, the term chosen is the 'experience industry' which includes tourism and restaurants. These two industries combined account for almost 40 per cent of the entire 'experience industry' in Sweden and make the definition quite different from many other nations' industry definitions (Almqvist & Dahl 2003). However, by using this definition it is possible to inflate the size of the 'experience industry'. Leif Pagrotsky, at the time Swedish Minister of Industry, explains how he thinks about these industries: 'They are all helping to put Sweden on the world map, to enhance the image of Sweden as a creative and forward-thinking country' (Pagrotsky 2003).

The term 'experience industry' stems from Pine and Gilmore (1998) and, according to the creators, it may include many business sectors including retailing, transportation, tourism, banking, media etc. Pine and Gilmore did not use the term experience *industry*, but referred to the experience *economy*. The experience economy is emphasizing *how* an activity is executed rather than *what* that activity is all about. The experience industry, which is based on this concept, may be a useful management approach or a potent tool to boost a region's image, but it is of less use as a tool in industry analyses.

'Creative industries' (Caves 2000; Hartley 2005; Howkins 2001) has during the last decade largely replaced 'cultural industries' as the most frequently used industry label, especially in Anglophone countries. It differs from 'experience industry' since it is not focused on *how* an activity is executed but on the *input* required for that execution. However, the problem with this term is almost the same as with 'experience industry': it is far too inclusive. Most definitions of the creative industries include architecture, design and fashion. The same arguments motivating the inclusion of these industries could be used for instance to include the consumer electronics industry, the automotive industry or the pharmaceutical industry where creativity also is of great importance. The scope of the definition is so wide that any attempt to produce knowledge which has validity across all the industries included becomes a futile endeavour. Proponents of the term answer this criticism by stating that creative processes are found across all industries, and it is not possible to define the 'creative industries' by their output, since it is focused upon the input of these processes (Hartley 2005:27). That claim is true indeed, but industries are not defined by input, or by the manner in which activities are performed. Industries are defined by the goods or services produced or supplied.

It is certainly true that creativity is an important part of many industries, perhaps it is even of growing importance to the entire economy, but, once again, it is questionable whether creativity is a useful label to delineate a part of the economy in order to facilitate structured analysis. The shortcomings of the term 'creative or experience industries' have during recent years been increasingly recognized by several scholars in the field. There is a growing tendency to rather link the prefix 'creative' to concepts of 'economy', 'class' or 'citizen' rather than to 'industry' (e.g. Florida 2002; Hartley 2007) – a practice which is by far more useful and relevant.

Yet another term which also deserves some attention is the term 'media industries'. Ferguson (2006:297), Hadenius and Weibull (2003) and Picard (2002:12–17) all give the term a meaning which is very similar to 'cultural industries' but nevertheless there are some minor differences between the various definitions. Traditionally, the (mass) media industries include the newspaper, magazine, radio and television industries (e.g. Hadenius & Weibull 2003). However, due to the evolution of these industries the definition of what is and what is not part of the media industries has been challenged. The 'Internet industry' is now often included, and other scholars choose to include book, film, videogame, music and advertising in the definition (Ferguson 2006; Picard 2002) – in other words, a definition which is almost identical to Hesmondhalgh's listing of the core cultural industries (2002:12).

The list of suggested terms which might be used to label the music industry continues and includes rather exotic terms such as the 'sunrise industries'! However, rather than using any of the terms discussed above, I believe a useful way to categorize the music industry is to consider it as a *copyright* industry. Copyright legislation is what makes it possible to commodify a musical work, be it a song, an arrangement, a recording etc. The core of the music industry is about 'developing musical content and personalities' (Negus 1992), and to be able to license the use of that content and those personalities to consumers and businesses they need to be protected by copyright legislation.

The use of this term is not new in any way, but has been used by several institutions, for instance OECD (2005b), IFPI (2004a), Congress of the United States (CBO 2004) and of course by the WIPO. I argue that by considering the popular music industry as a copyright industry rather than a cultural or a creative industry I emphasize the nature of the products that are created and traded within that industry. The term also has a clearer definition and is less ambiguous than many of the other terms, which makes it more useful during analyses of the dynamics of these firms and industries.

Now when I have categorized the music industry as a copyright industry, a number of important questions need to be addressed, such as: What features characterize this kind of industry? What do I already know about the behaviour of the copyright industry?

What approach should be used in order to be able to explain the dynamics of these industries in the digital age? Let us first start with the basic concepts of copyright.

Basic concepts of copyright

The 'Statute of Anne' is generally considered to be the world's earliest copyright legislation. This English law which went into force in 1710 marks a shift from a system where printers were able to print books without compensating the authors for their creative labour to a system where *authors* would have the exclusive right to reproduce books. The Act explains its background and purpose:

> Whereas Printers, Booksellers, and other Persons, have of late frequently taken the Liberty of Printing, Reprinting, and Publishing, or causing to be Printed, Reprinted, and Published Books, and other Writings, without the Consent of the Authors or Proprietors of such Books and Writings, to their very great Detriment, and too often to the Ruin of them and their Families: For Preventing therefore such Practices for the future, and for the Encouragement of Learned Men to Compose and Write useful Books . . .

The copyright legislation was from the beginning a national law which only covered literary works, but over the centuries the legislation expanded to include paintings, drawings, music etc. It also expanded to provide protection not only for a nation's own artists but for all artists, regardless of their origin and nationality. The most important legislation in international copyright law is the Berne Convention, from 1886. It was the French author Victor Hugo who was the strongest proponent for recognizing authors' rights internationally, which eventually resulted in the Berne Convention. Over the years, the Convention has been developed and expanded in order to recognize a number of copyright-related features which now are considered as fundamental and crucial in international copyright legislation – for instance that no formalities shall be required in order for there to be a copyright, i.e. it is not necessary to register a song for it to be protected (Article 5: Rights Guaranteed). Since 1948, the Convention also governs 'additional rights' in order to respond to new technologies, such as sound recording technology (Article 9: Right of Reproduction). The Berne Convention also introduced the concept of moral rights, i.e. the right to be recognized as author, and for one's work not to be subject to derogatory treatment: 'Independently of the author's economic rights, and even after the transfer of the said rights, the author shall have the right to claim authorship of the work and to object to any distortion, mutilation or other modification of, or other derogatory action in relation to, the said work, which would be prejudicial to his honor or reputation'. (The Berne Convention – Article 6bis: Moral Rights).

The moral right is an example of how copyright-related legislations differ between countries, even though it is an international legislation. In many countries with a 'civil law legal system' (which is the predominant legal system in the world), the right to be recognized as the author of a creative work is an inalienable right – it cannot be transferred, bought or sold. This is often not the case in countries with a 'common law legal system' (primarily nations which trace their legal heritage to Britain, including the UK, the USA, and other former colonies of the British Empire). In these countries, the moral right is considered to be similar to the copyright and can be bought or sold like any other commodity. The regulatory differences between countries have implications for contracts signed between parties in the music industry, and any other copyright industry for that matter. In some countries, the moral rights can be covered by the contract while in other countries they cannot. In order to cope with this 'difficulty' in civil law countries, it is common that artists agree not to enforce their moral rights, even if they will formally still have them.

The Berne Convention was originally a European instrument, but since 1989 when the USA signed the Convention, and since 1994 when the TRIPS (Trade-Related Aspects of Intellectual Property Rights) Agreement made the Convention a mandatory part of general international trade agreements, the Convention has confirmed its position as the most important treaty within the realm of international copyright (MacQueen, Waelde & Laurie 2007:38).

The significance of international copyright legislation continues to grow as the society moves further into the digital age. New treaties are signed and copyright legislation is one of the most discussed and controversial areas of international law. Among the important treaties which have come into force during the last two decades is the World International Property Organization's Internet Treaty from 1996. This treaty served as the basis for national and regional legislations such as the Digital Millennium Copyright Act (DMCA) in the USA and the European Union Copyright Directive (EUCD) in Europe, which will be further discussed in chapter 5. Another controversial treaty within the European Union is the Directive on the Enforcement of Intellectual Property Rights (IPRED) which came into force during 2004.

Characteristics of the copyright industries

There are several characteristics of the copyright industries that make them different from 'non-copyright' industries (see e.g. Caves 2000:2–10; Chan-Olmsted 2006:173; Hesmondhalgh 2002). Some of these characteristics will be discussed in this section.

On the nature of copyright products

As I noted earlier in this chapter, Hirsch defined cultural products as 'nonmaterial goods directed at a public of consumers, for whom they generally serve an aesthetic or expressive, rather than utilitarian function' (1972:641). In addition to being 'nonmaterial', cultural products have some specific properties that differentiate them from products traded in many other industries.

First of all, the products traded in copyright industries are often categorized as *information goods* simply because they are

Denisoff (1975) referred to it as 'the buckshot theory' when he explored the music publishing industry. Following this strategy, a considerable number of contracts are signed. By monitoring how consumers react to the songs, the company is able to focus its resources on those products the audiences seem to like.

Following this practice, a staggering amount of new copyright products are released annually. Data on how many new titles (books, music albums, magazines, movies, videogames etc.) are annually released worldwide are not readily available, but at least 1,000,000 books were published worldwide during 2002 (Zaid 2003), and at least 100,000 music albums were released worldwide during 2004 (IFPI 2004b). Hesmondhalgh (2002) refers to Neuman (1991:139) when claiming that 80 per cent of the revenues in the book publishing industry stems from 20 per cent of the portfolio, and to Wolf (1999:89) when claiming that only 2 per cent of music albums sold in the US during 1998 sold more than 50,000 copies. In other words, it is this small percentage that support all the other titles that are unable to deliver acceptable earnings.

High production costs, low reproduction costs

The dominant portion of the costs in copyright industries is attributed to the production of 'the first copy' and the marketing of the title in question. This is to say that, once the first copy or the design has been made, most of the project costs have been paid. Two observations can be made about these costs. First, they are mainly *fixed*, that is to say they are independent of the number of products sold. Second, they are usually considered as *sunk costs*, that is to say they are paid before the products are available to the public and are not recoverable, even if the project is immediately halted (Hesmondhalgh 2002; Picard 2002; Shapiro & Varian 1999; Vogel 2001).

The cost structure in the copyright industries has considerable effects on the behaviour of copyright firms, primarily since it 'leads to considerable economies of scale, i.e. the more you produce, the lower your average cost of production' (Shapiro &

intangible and 'can be digitized' (Shapiro & Varian 1999:3). It is important to note what actually is traded on copyright markets. When people purchase a vase or a CD, they do not purchase the design of the vase or the copyrights to the sound recording. The only thing purchased is an example of the vase design or a right to listen to the sound recording within certain carefully defined restrictions. Only very few are able actually to *own* music, since full and exclusive copyright of a single commercially successful song is most likely far beyond the financial constraints of the average consumer.

The agreement between the rights holder and the consumer governs how the latter is allowed to use, for instance, a sound recording. This degree of freedom is often referred to as the product's 'option value' (Shapiro & Varian 1999). If an information product has a high option value, the restrictions on the consumers' ability to use the product are relatively relaxed, and vice versa. A rented DVD has a lower option value than a purchased DVD. A song distributed via broadcast radio has lower option value than a song distributed on a CD or compact cassette.

Copyright products are often referred to as *experience products* since consumers generally are unable to determine whether a book, a film or a song is good or not, until they have read the book, seen the film or heard the song, respectively (e.g. Hoskins & McFadyen 2004:76–8).[7] Promotion of experience products is often based on the ability to distribute the product with a lower option value. For instance, demo versions of computer software are information goods with limited option value, which is supposed to create a demand for the same product, but with a higher option value. Traditional promotion of popular music is based on the same logic. By playing the song on broadcast radio (low option value) the record company is hoping that a demand is generated for the same information, but with a higher option value, for instance as distributed on a CD.

Experience products are closely linked to *time*, basically because it takes time to experience something. The audience also has to make priorities between which copyright products should be

awarded their attention. For instance it is not possible to experience every new song released, since there simply isn't enough
time. This phenomenon is described in Herbert Simon's words:
'What information consumes is rather obvious: it consumes the
attention of its recipients. Hence, a wealth of information creates a poverty of attention, and a need to allocate that attention
efficiently among the overabundance of information sources that
might consume it' (Simon 1971:40).

The audience is consequently unable to make well-informed
decisions regarding its consumption of copyright products. In
the case of music, the audience is only able to experience a fraction of the total number of new products released in the market.[8]
Compare this for instance to the refrigerator market, where
consumers are in a much better position to be well informed
about the available options. They can compare different retailers'
prices and make a rational decision based on solid information.
Hirsch describes the completely different situation in the copyright industries: 'In all [such] industries, the number of already
available goods far exceeds the number that can be successfully
marketed. More goods are produced and available than actually
reach the consumer' (Hirsch 1970:5). In order to cope with this
situation, structures have emerged in most copyright industries
which Hirsch refers to as 'preselection systems'. The purpose
of the preselection systems is to reduce the number of available
products in order to facilitate the audience's decision-making.
The preselection system consists of a number of subsystems,
and the members of the different subsystems, the gatekeepers,
determine whether the product shall pass through the filtering
process or not.[9]

An industry with a high level of uncertainty and volatility
The level of uncertainty and risk in the copyright industries is
highlighted by many scholars. Negus ponders about uncertainty
in the music industry: 'I found much uncertainty among person-
nel involved in producing music. Neither business executives,
fans, the musicians themselves nor journalists can predict what

is going to be commercially successful or what new musics are
going to be critically acclaimed' (Negus 1996:48). Hirsch also
notes how members of a preselection system have limited ability to 'predict accurately which of the items produced will pass
successfully through each stage of the complex filter' (Hirsch
1970:5). Other scholars, for instance, Caves (2000), Hartley
(2005), Hoskins & McFadyen (2004) and Picard (2002) make
similar observations.

There are several ways to explain this exceptional condition.
First, the development and release of new products, regardless
of industry, always involve a high level of risk and uncertainty. In
most industries it is difficult to forecast whether a new product
will be successful or not. However, the potential success of a copyright product is even more difficult to predict than that of other
non-copyright products. If the product category is reasonably
established in the market, consumers are able to determine
whether they would be interested in a new product which follows
a certain set of specifications. But a copyright product can only
be evaluated by the consumer after 'the first copy' has been produced. Only then (maybe) is market research of any relevance.
Second, the consumption of copyright products is highly volatile
and unpredictable (Picard 2002:7–9). 'Fashionable performers
or styles, even if heavily marketed, can suddenly come to be
perceived as outmoded, and other texts can become unexpectedly successful' (Hesmondhalgh 2002:18). Combine these two
observations and a situation emerges where it is extremely difficult to gain information about the potential success of a coming
release. Consequently, decision-makers in copyright firms often
have to make decisions about how to spend their investment
monies based on intuition and gut feeling. One common way
of dealing with such a high exposure to risk is to use the principles of portfolio theory (Picard 2002; 2005; Reca 2006). Risk is
reduced by investing in several diverse markets and products, in
the hope that aggregate return from these investments at least
will attain some degree of stability. Hesmondhalgh (2002) refers
to this strategy as 'throwing mud' in order to see what sticks.

Varian 1999:21). This means that while it may require a considerable number of items sold before profitability is achieved, the
profitability beyond the point of break-even may be substantial.
This logic 'leads to a very strong orientation towards audience
maximisation in the [copyright] industries' (Hesmondhalgh
2002:19). In other words, it makes much more economic sense
to sell a single title to a large audience rather than to sell the same
number of items, but distributed across ten different titles.

Profit maximization, creativity and authenticity

An interesting aspect of the copyright industries is the apparent
conflict between art and commerce. In this section I introduce
some of the basic concepts and bring the debate to the music
industrial context.

Firms are economic entities which acquire and organize
resources in order to produce goods and services (Picard 2002: 2).
According to the neoclassical economic theory usually referred to
as *the theory of the firm*, the objective of a firm is to maximize profit
and shareholder value (e.g. Hoskins & McFadyen 2004:141; Picard
2002:3). Profit is usually defined as 'the money that remains
after expenses are subtracted from income' (Picard 2002:4).
Shareholder value is assumed to be created through share price
appreciation and dividends in combination (Knight 1998:21).

According to this reasoning, economic value is the end, and
the activities taking place within the firm are merely means in
achieving that end. It is not particularly important whether those
activities are generating milkshakes or movies, as long as they are
delivering profit. However, though there may be entrepreneurs
and managers who subscribe to this perspective, many entrepreneurs in the copyright industries are motivated by something
else, beyond profit and economic value (Brulin & Nilsson 1997).
The business is an evil necessity, and the creative process, not
the profit, is the single and ultimate objective (Karlsson & Lekvall
2002). Regardless of these priorities, there are very few symbol
creators who are able to disregard economic realities completely.

Any venture has to be able to pay the bills, make improvements in facilities, have access to capital markets, experiment with new methods and so on; otherwise the venture will eventually vanish. Most copyright entrepreneurs quickly conclude that a 'firm' is a convenient way to structure their ventures – the practising of their craft. By establishing a firm they are able to enter business agreements with other economic entities; they are able to compete for external funding for various projects; they can regulate various uncertainties; they are able to attract talent; and so on (e.g. Coase 1937). Consequently, any firm, regardless of if it is operating in a copyright industry or not, has to deliver some kind of profit. It may be that it is not entirely necessary to *maximize* profit, but rather to deliver *good enough* profits which allow the symbol creators to continue practising their craft as long as they are able to keep their spirits burning.

The reasoning above assumes the firm in question is small and that the owners and managers are the same individuals. This is probably a fair representation of most firms operating in the copyright industries, including the music industry (e.g. Karlsson & Lekvall 2002:11). As the copyright firm evolves, it generates profits that can be accumulated in the firm and used for various future projects. Some larger projects might nevertheless require additional capital, for instance the production of a movie or the investment in new studio facilities. In these instances, the smaller copyright firm might turn to a bank to borrow additional capital (Picard 2002:172). This allows the firm access to capital without giving up the control of the firm. However, larger copyright firms have for many years turned to the public stock markets to get access to capital.[10] The larger firms require considerable financial resources to support their investments in expensive technologies, expansions into new territories etc. A publicly traded firm has considerably better access to capital compared with an unlisted firm. In addition, the firm is able to use its own shares as currency, which facilitates mergers with and acquisitions of other firms.

Firms listed for trade on a public stock market get access to capital in exchange for ownership of the firm. Although there are many pros in having access to a public stock market, there are also some considerable cons. When listed on a public stock market, the firm is constantly scrutinized by investors who are comparing the financial performance of the firm with every other investment opportunity available. Since the deregulation and internationalization of the financial markets during the last two or three decades, these investment opportunities may range from real estate in Moscow to Mexican bio-tech companies, Scandinavian hedge funds and literally thousands of other objects (e.g. Albarran & Chan-Olmsted 1998; Castells 1996; Picard 2002:185). If the copyright firm is unable to avoid below-average financial performance in comparison to the other options, investors will simply move their monies elsewhere. When this happens, Adam Smith's invisible hand will lower the share price until investors again will regard the shares as good value for money. This logic puts the publicly traded copyright firm in a situation where the decision regarding what profits are *good enough* is determined by the international financial market rather than by the management of the firm. The firm has to deliver maximum profits to satisfy the shareholders' quest for highest possible return on investment, otherwise the future of the firm is jeopardized. In other words, when a firm is listed for trade on a public stock market, the only profit good enough is the maximum (Knight 1998; Picard 2002).

A note from the evolutionary economist is required here. Claiming that the firm's goal is profit maximization is *not* to claim that the firm makes continuous rational decisions which are maximizing profit. As Cyert and March (1992 [1963]) noted, the decision-making process is complex, and often the firm's decisions are not rational and not at all based on correct, unbiased information.

Authenticity and creativity
Is it really possible to create 'authentic art' in organizations where profit maximization is one of the most important goals?

Can truly creative processes exist under such circumstances? Following the reasoning of Horkheimer, Adorno and their disciples, the combination is simply impossible (Adorno 1941; Horkheimer & Adorno 1944). To achieve authenticity, culture should be created by a symbol creator who is independent of any commercial pressure. Those who choose to be associated with the 'majors', major commercial institutions in the copyright industries, are sell-outs or victims, depending on perspective. Negus (1996:46) comments on this way of understanding the music industry: 'On one side are the heroes – the musicians, producers and performers (the creative artists); opposing them are the villains – the record companies and entertainment corporations (the commercial corrupters and manipulators).'

The concept of the 'major' deserves some further attention. 'A major' is usually the term used to represent a large copyright firm with operations in several countries and in control of a well-established distribution machinery. The major is usually publicly traded or is a part of an entertainment conglomerate. This should be compared with 'independent (companies)' or 'indies', which usually are the opposite of everything above, and have a stronger focus on the text, the creativity and the art, rather than the commerce. The work created within the realms of an indie is considered to be less a part of the capitalistic system. Based on the logic of Adorno and others, it is also more 'authentic' than a work created within the walls of a major.

But what is authentic art? Another way of approaching the issue is to focus on creativity rather than trying to distinguish the 'authentic' from the 'fake'. The social psychologist Teresa Amabile has done extensive research on creativity within organizations (e.g. 1996; 1998). When defining creativity, she chooses to focus on the output: 'A product or response will be judged as creative to the extent that (a) it is both a novel and appropriate, useful, correct or valuable response to the task at hand, and (b) the task is heuristic rather than algorithmic' (Amabile 1996:35).

An important question then is whether the 'tasks' within copyright industries are heuristic or algorithmic.[11] Amabile reflects on this issue: '. . . an artist who followed the algorithm "paint pictures of different sorts of children with large sad eyes, using dark-toned backgrounds" would not be producing creative paintings, even if each painting were unique and technically perfect' (Amabile 1996:36). This is exactly what is happening in industrial production of culture according to the reasoning of the Frankfurt School. Symbol creators in the copyright industries follow 'an algorithm' in order to deliver products that fulfil certain criteria and hence are commercially successful in the marketplace (Adorno 1941).

Amabile concludes that individual creativity, to a large extent, is dependent on the person's social environment. She stresses the importance of finding your own, internal motivation and being able to stay independent of demands and reactions from the environment. A symbol creator's primary driver has to be the joy, will or need to *create for its own sake*, independent of whether the product will be received by good reviews or commercial success. Amabile summarizes her conclusions by stating that 'Intrinsic motivation is conductive to creativity, but extrinsic motivation is detrimental' (Amabile 1996:15).

Art and commerce in the music industry
Frith (e.g. 1978; 1983) has argued that there is no conflict between art and commerce, at least not in the music industry. Frith claims that rock music, which sometimes is considered as a musical genre with relatively high levels of authenticity, was not created outside the system of commercial music. Rather rock music was created within that system, and is a result of combining creativity and commerce. Building on this analysis, Frith concluded that the relationship between art and commerce should not be described as antagonistic, but rather as integrated. Negus has challenged Frith by pointing to the actual experiences of audiences and artists: 'If those of us who study popular music are to take seriously the vocabularies of participants, [. . .] then

the use of clichés [. . .] in discussions about the music industry cannot simply be dismissed as artistic conceit or audience naïveté' (Negus 1996:47). One such artist who very explicitly explained his feelings of being trapped within the capitalistic system and unable to express his creativity is Prince Roger Nelson regarding his former record label[12] Warner Bros (e.g. Mitchell 2005; Orwall 1995; Rosen 1994). Prince performed several times with the word 'slave' written on his forehead as a way of describing his relationship with his employer. If the words of Prince and many other symbol creators are taken seriously, there apparently is some kind of tension between art and commerce which contrasts the copyright industries with other industries.

Burnett (1990) and other scholars have shown that creative cultural production normally does not take place in large, mature organizations. Rather, it is the smaller firms ('the indies') which are able to create an environment where creativity is intrinsically motivated. Within the domains of popular music, this is confirmed over and over again, as new genres are developed or picked up by the smaller firm long before any larger firm has discovered the novelty. Apparently, the milieu within smaller firms is able to nourish a greater level of creativity than the milieu within larger firms. It has already been discussed in this text how the larger firm has to be more focused on profit maximization than the smaller firm. In addition, the larger firm requires more complex administration, including strategies, budgets, marketing plans, financial reports etc. All these structures create a whole range of external demands and restrictions. Where the small firm is driven forward by the joy of independence and the pleasure of creating something new (intrinsic motivation), the larger firm is primarily driven forward by the need to fulfil the next financial plan (extrinsic motivation).

In order to answer this problem, many larger music companies have created organizational structures which aim to establish a social environment within the firm which allows creativity to flourish, although the external demands remain in place. One such initiative is to establish 'semi-independent' business units within the larger firms (Burnett 1990). These smaller intra-organizational units are given a considerable amount of freedom in order to let the intrinsic motivation guide the organization forward. Hesmondhalgh points to a similar strategy within the copyright industries when he refers to the 'loose control of symbol creators' within copyright industries, which is motivated by the 'long-standing assumptions about the ethical desirability of creative autonomy, which derive from the romantic conception of symbolic creativity, and traditions of free speech' (Hesmondhalgh 2002:22).

Let us now continue with another question which is of vital importance in our attempt at understanding the music industry as a copyright industry. What approach should be used and what tools are needed in order to explore the dynamics of a copyright industry?

Exploring copyright industry dynamics

Exploring copyright industry dynamics basically means exploring the development of a phenomenon during an extended period of time, rather than at a specific moment. I ask questions such as what kind of change can be observed? What are the drivers of this change, and how does the change in turn affect other parts of the phenomenon? The unit of analysis is primarily the organization, or, more specifically, the music firm. However, I am also interested in how change occurs on an individual level, such as how roles and responsibilities within an organization evolve over time. As revealed by the title of this book and this section, I am also interested in how the change at individual and organizational levels interplays with dynamics on an industrial level.

The microenvironment of the copyright firm
One classic model for analysing how the industrial environment influences a firm's ability to grow and survive was suggested by

Michael Porter in 1980. The model uses concepts from industrial organization economics[13] to derive five 'forces', which together constitute the microenvironment where a firm is operating. Based on an understanding of this environment, managers are able to make strategic decisions regarding where to manoeuvre their organization in order to create competitive advantage. The five forces are presented and briefly discussed below.

1 Threat of new entrants – barriers to entry and mobility   Is it likely that new or existing companies enter the market with competing products or services? The threat of new entrants may be determined by several different factors. One such factor may be *capital requirements*, for instance the financing needed to establish operations and pay start-up losses (Picard 2002:72). A second potential factor is *product differentiation*; for instance, if existing firms already have unique products with great consumer loyalty, a new firm will have difficulty in getting a foothold in the market. A third factor is what is known as *switching costs*, for instance if consumers have acquired a content library from a supplier using a specific media technology, it will be costly for the consumer to switch to another supplier which is using another, competing technology. Depending on your perspective and specific situation, this mechanism may be referred to as *lock-in* and is a well-established strategy in many industries (e.g. Hax & Wilde 2001; Shapiro & Varian 1999).[14] Limited *access to distribution channels*, for instance the limited shelf space available for the display of magazines, is also a factor that is determining the barriers to entry. A new player might for instance be unable to gain access to that shelf space, which will make it difficult to enter the market. Finally, *governmental regulations* may be a barrier to entry if they, for instance, restrict access to the frequency spectrum available for terrestrial broadcasting.

2 Substitutability of products or services   How great is the risk that buyers replace the current product or service with something else, which satisfies the same need, but in a different way? In the copyright industries, products are normally relatively differentiated and the level of substitutability and competition between them is limited. A cheering U2 fan is not very likely to substitute Bono with another artist without great reluctance. The customer loyalty that can be found within the music industry is often looked at with envy by actors operating in other industries. However, as with most of the forces in Porter's model, substitutability may vary between different parts of a value chain. The same content may for instance be distributed using a number of different media technologies (e.g. VHS, DVD and BitTorrent). Even though the substitutability on content level is low, the substitutability and level of competition between different distribution technologies may be fierce.

3 & 4 Bargaining power of buyers and suppliers   Are the buyers able to negotiate a lower price, improved quality etc., or are they restricted to accepting whatever is offered? In consumer-oriented businesses, the bargaining power of buyers is generally low. It is not particularly easy to negotiate a lower ticket price at the box office. The corresponding reasoning can be directed towards suppliers. Are the suppliers strong enough to demand higher prices, better contractual terms etc., or are the suppliers restricted to accepting whatever terms are offered by the players in the industry? There are many different kinds of suppliers to a music firm, but if the focus is set on the artist, the bargaining power depends heavily on the artist's previous success. The new and unknown artist has a bargaining power which is close to zero. If the artist wants to get international and physical distribution, there are few other options than to aim for a contract with one of the majors. The terms of these contracts are usually dictated by the record label and accepted by the artist. At the other end of the spectrum is the megastar who is able to act quite differently. During the last couple of years, there have been several cases where a record label has signed agreements where the firm has taken a large portion of the business risk and a minor portion of the expected profit (e.g. EMI 2002b).

5 Rivalry among firms already operating in the market How intense is the competition between existing actors in the industry? The competition between firms is to a great extent linked to the structure of the industry. Neoclassical economic theory defines a market-structure continuum ranging from *monopoly* to *oligopoly, monopolistic competition* and finally to *perfect competition* (e.g. Hoskins & McFadyen 2004; Wildman 2006:72–5). Perfect competition is the condition where a considerable number of equally sized firms compete with identical products. Consumers are also numerous and have complete and correct information regarding the products and prices offered by the firms competing on the market. Under these conditions, price is usually the only competitive weapon. However, this condition is not relevant to the copyright industries: 'Markets for information will not, and *cannot*, look like textbook-perfect competitive markets in which there are many suppliers offering similar products, each lacking the ability to influence prices' (Shapiro & Varian 1999:23). Monopolistic competition is somewhat more realistic than perfect competition, since the products offered are differentiated rather than identical. In this kind of market, it is possible to compete by using product innovation, rather than by price only. Oligopoly is an industry dominated by few large firms producing differentiated products. Under these conditions the barriers to entry are usually substantial. The competition between these large players is consequently lower than in the previous two cases. Copyright industries such as music, movie and broadcasting are best described as oligopolies (e.g. Hoskins & McFadyen 2004; Picard 2002). Finally, monopoly is an industry with a single player, and consequently no rivalry at all.

An evolutionary theory of the firm

The five-forces model is useful when decision-makers carve out the firm's strategy. Early strategy scholars (e.g. Ansoff 1965; Bain 1959) often understand a firm's 'strategy' as a formalized set of rules for making decisions. The decision rules can also be seen

as a *position* which is to be assumed based on where the organization is today and where it wants to be within a certain period of
time. Several scholars have followed this school of thought. For
instance, Porter explained strategy as the firm's position taken
after the investigation of the competitive environment (Porter
1980). According to Porter, there are only two ways a firm can
compete: either by focusing on low cost or by focusing on product differentiation. It is not possible to combine the two options
successfully (Porter 1980).

A different way of thinking about strategy was suggested by
Birger Wernerfelt. While Porter emphasizes external factors,
Wernerfelt (1984) argues that the basis for a firm's competitive
advantage primarily lies in the firm's ability to develop, sustain
and apply a bundle of valuable resources. Resources should
in this context be understood as the firm's assets, capabilities,
routines, processes, skills, knowledge etc. (e.g. Barney 1991;
Wernerfelt 1984).

During the 1990s, strategy scholars added to this body of
research by recognizing the increasing volatility and uncertainty
in many industries. This turned the focus of organizational
theorists from questions regarding which strategic position is
most appropriate during a specific environmental condition,
to a firm's ability to *assume* new strategic positions as swiftly as
possible. Competition is not as much a 'war of position' as it is
a 'war of movement' (e.g. Ghemawat 1991; Hamel & Prahalad
1993; Porter 1991; Stalk 1988; Stalk, Evans and Shulman 1992;
Sterman 1994).

Building on Wernerfelt's resource-based view of the firm, the
concept of 'movements' translates into a question of how a firm
is able continuously to revise and develop its resources and capabilities in order to adapt to a volatile and uncertain environment.
This question, applied to the music industrial context, lies at the
core of this book. I examine how digital technologies affect the
production, promotion, distribution and consumption of music
and reveal how the music business is being fundamentally transformed in order to survive in a digital age.

Previous research into this field has to a large extent been based on the works by Nelson and Winter (1982) on organizational routines; by Cohen and Levinthal (1990) on absorptive capacity; by Teece, Pisano and Shuen (1997) on dynamic capabilities; by Argyris & Schön (1978) on organizational learning, or on some other similar framework. What is common to all these frameworks is that they rest on other basic microeconomic assumptions than many older theories, including Porter's five-forces model. The frameworks all rely on evolutionary economic theory rather than on neoclassical economic theory. Since evolutionary economics is fundamental to the perspective I am using in this book I shall look into what differentiates this theory from its ancestors and relatives.

Evolutionary concepts in economic theory started to emerge in the beginning of the twentieth century as an answer to a growing discomfort with the established neoclassical economic models. There are several problems with neoclassical economic models which, according to evolutionary economists, make them 'barren and irrelevant as an apparatus of thought' (Kaldor 1972:1237). One is that they focus heavily on equilibrium, optimum and static structures and do not actually describe the complex dynamics of an economy. If change occurs in neoclassical economic models, it occurs only within the given and static structures. In addition, neoclassical economics is generally based on the assumption that organizations and individuals make well-informed, rational decisions in order to maximize their financial wealth.

Evolutionary economists argue that the assumptions of neoclassical economic theory make it difficult to explain actual economic behaviour. Societal and economic systems are often *not* in equilibrium, and socio-economic structures *do* change, sometimes even rather dramatically. Also, individuals and organizations are often unable to make well-informed decisions, and, often, these decisions are biased and irrational, contrary to neoclassical economic theory (e.g. England 1994; Simon 1979).

Evolutionary economics is often linked to Darwin's publishing of *On the Origin of Species* in 1859. 'Darwinian' change differs from non-evolutionary 'Newtonian' change in that the first is caused by changes in system structure, while the latter represents change within a given structure (Hamilton 1953). The distinction can be used to differentiate economic growth (more of the same) from economic development (structural change) (Boulding 1981). During the twentieth century several scholars continued to mould the framework of evolutionary economics. Many aspects of Joseph Schumpeter's reasoning are evolutionary in their character. His model of innovation and economic change is probably the most apparent example (1911) but also in his discussions regarding Marxist economic theory, his inkling towards evolutionary economics is apparent: 'The essential point is that in dealing with capitalism I are dealing with an evolutionary process. It may seem strange that anyone can fail to see so obvious a fact which moreover was long ago emphasized by Karl Marx' (Schumpeter 1942:82). Other scholars (e.g. Nelson & Winter 1982; Radzicki & Sterman 1994) have continued to contribute to the field by adding other metaphors and concepts to the framework. Myrdal (1956) introduced the theory of circular and cumulative causation and Boulding (e.g. 1968; 1978; 1981) applied the second law of thermodynamics and the concepts of time irreversibility to the analysis of economic systems. Others contributed with theories of self-organization, complexity and chaos to explain organizations' adaptive processes (e.g. Foster & Metcalfe 2001; Lorenz 1989; Radzicki 1990; Varian 1979; Witt 2003).

Further, March and Simon (1958) and Cyert and March (1992 [1963]) used an evolutionary approach when they developed the *behavioural theory of the firm*. They explained intra-organizational decision-making by using the concept of bounded rationality, i.e. the fact that decision-makers are not well-informed and rational, but sometimes pretty far from that description. This understanding of organizational decision-making can be traced further to the models of organizational learning presented for instance by Argyris and Schön (1978) and later by Senge (1990).

The process of organizational adaptation
Like many other organizational theorists working in the spirit of
evolutionary economic theory, Miles and Snow (1978) observed
that different organizations react differently to environmental
change. They suggested a simple typology consisting of four
types of organization (defenders, prospectors, analysers and
reactors), each with its own way of adapting to environmental
change (Miles & Snow 1978:30).

Defenders are organizations which are producing a limited
set of products directed at a narrow segment of the market.
Their most important strategic question is how to produce and
distribute goods and services as efficiently as possible. The
management team of the defender is usually dominated by production and cost-control specialists and has little or no expertise
focused on scanning the environment for new product or market
opportunities. Since these firms have chosen this organizational
structure, their greatest risk is that of being unable to respond to
a major shift in their environment. Consequently, the defender
strategy and structure is most viable in stable industries, such as
mining or food-processing (Miles & Snow 1978; Miles, Snow,
Meyer & Coleman 1978)

Prospectors are organizations which in many respects are the
opposite of the defenders. Their prime capability is that of finding and exploiting new product and market opportunities. The
prospectors' domain of markets and products is usually broad
and in a continuous state of development. They are frequently
the creators of change in their industries, and change and innovation are often their major tools in gaining an edge over their
competitors. For prospectors, the reputation as an innovator
is as important as, perhaps even more important than, high
profitability. In fact, because of this prioritization and the inevi-
table 'failure rate' associated with sustained product and market
innovation, prospectors may find it difficult to consistently reach
the profit levels of the more efficient defenders (Miles & Snow
1978).

While defenders and prospectors reside at opposite ends of

a continuum of adaptation strategies, the *analyser* is the balanced combination of the two extremes. A true analyser is an organization that attempts to minimize risk while maximizing the opportunity for profit. To achieve this aim, analysers usually operate in several product-market domains, some relatively stable, others changing. In their stable areas, these organizations operate routinely and efficiently through use of formalized structures and processes. In their more turbulent areas, top managers watch their competitors closely for new ideas, and then rapidly adopt those which appear to be the most promising (Miles & Snow 1978).

The fourth type, the *reactor*, is not really an adaptation strategy, but rather the lack thereof. An organization of this type acts inconsistently and seldom makes adjustments of any sort until it is absolutely forced to do so by environmental pressures. Unless the organization is operating in a monopolistic or highly regulated industry, it cannot continue to behave as a reactor indefinitely. Sooner or later, it must move towards one of the consistent and stable strategies of defender, analyser or prospector (Miles & Snow 1978).

Previously I have recognized that the music industry is both a volatile and chaotic environment. Based on that observation combined with the reasoning of Miles and Snow, one might argue that in the music industry, the 'prospector-like' firm has a much greater sustainability than the 'defender-like' firm.

Communities of practice
Evolutionary economic theory generally has a firm-level or industry-level focus on dynamic processes and is very useful when exploring how music firms have evolved together with the industry in which they operate. However, I am also interested in aspects on an individual level, in addition to those on firm or industry level. In that endeavour, I turn to the Communities of Practice (CoP) framework which originates from the works of Lave and Wenger (1991), and has been brought to the mainstream of organizational theory by Brown and Duguid (1991).

Although they have different intellectual heritages – economics and social learning theories – Evolutionary Economics and Communities of Practice have been applied to investigate somewhat similar organizational problems, such as how what people in organizations do (routines, practice) impacts organizational outcomes.

Wenger defines a Community of Practice as a 'group of people who share a concern or a passion for something they do and learn how to do it better as they interact regularly' (Wenger 2006). Wenger also notes that not all communities are a Community of Practice, and that three characteristics have to be fulfilled:

- *A domain.* Members of a CoP do not necessarily have to know each other but they have to share an interest and passion in a certain domain. The domain can, for instance, be based on a certain musical instrument or genre.
- *A community.* The members must engage in activities which allow them to learn from each other. Various kinds of media can support such activities, for example magazines or websites. However, it is important to note that an online community in itself does not automatically qualify as a CoP.
- *A practice.* A CoP is indeed a community of practitioners and not a community of interest. It is not enough to have a shared interest; the members of a CoP develop certain skills, experiences and tools which they actively use in their practice (Wenger 2006).

The CoP framework tries to explain how norms, values, beliefs, routines evolve in a Community of Practice. How does an individual learn what is the right way of doing things, what it actually means to be a music producer, etc.? How does collective knowledge develop within a Community of Practice? According to CoP, these norms and structures are continuously constructed through a learning process in which individual 'learners do not receive or even construct abstract, "objective", individual knowledge; rather they learn to function in a community . . . They acquire that particular community's subjective viewpoint and

learn to speak its language. In short, they are "enculturated"'
(Brown, Collins & Duguid 1989).

Production of culture
The frameworks and theories discussed so far have a heritage
in economic and organizational theory and treat the copyright
industries as an economic activity like most other economic
activities. These frameworks are indeed potent tools for analysing the new music economy. However, it is also important to
enrich the theoretical toolbox with frameworks which consider
music, movies, videogames, books etc. first and foremost as
cultural artefacts which in various ways interact with society, and
secondly as commodities aimed for trade and consumption.

One theoretical lens with such an emphasis is literary studies, or its relatives, musicology, film studies, cultural studies etc.
However, although literary studies and the rest may be useful
frameworks when exploring culture, it will not be used in this
study, since I am not focused on the musical products *per se*, but
rather *how* and *why* these products are produced. Instead, I have
found what I need in the field of the sociology of culture.

The studying of popular culture within the field of sociology
can be traced back to the first half of the last century (e.g. Weber
1921; Adorno 1941), but it has only been considered as a serious topic since the 1970s (Dowd 2002; Hirsch & Fiss 2000;
Peterson 2000). Earlier, 'mass culture' could perhaps be studied
as a social problem, but the 'culture industry' was not considered
to be a relevant topic for research. During the 1970s, a young
breed of sociologists began to approach culture and the organizations where culture is produced. These researchers tried to
'de-politicize' the topic by treating it less as a social concern and
more as just another challenge for economic and organizational
analysts (Hirsch & Fiss 2000).

One of these sociologists, Richard Peterson, charted new
ground in the article 'Cycles in Symbol Production: The Case
of Popular Music', published with David Berger in *American
Sociological Review* in 1975 (Peterson & Berger 1975). In this

article, Peterson and Berger explored copyright industry dynamics by linking the level of industry concentration within the music industry to the diversity of cultural output. Based on their empirical material, covering twenty-six years, they were able to conclude that a high level of concentration causes a low level of diversity and vice versa. Hirsch and Fiss recognize the importance of that article.

> It opened the door to enabling sociologists to analyze the popular arts descriptively and non-pejoratively, leaving the normative and critical aspects to other fields. In keeping with the discipline's focus of that time, here was a connection to social structure and markets, but no longer critical of its capitalistic framework, and enabling the field to approach aesthetics without judging their quality. In fact, the content or quality of the product is irrelevant, or simply a 'matter of taste' that remains external to the framework. Whether leisure time is spent on wrestling matches or opera or baseball is immaterial. (Hirsch & Fiss 2000:100)

Building on the seminal article, Peterson (e.g. 1976; 1979; 1982; 1985) developed the 'production of culture' perspective which since has become a significant part of production-related research within the sociology of culture. Peterson challenged the notion that cultural products are 'the work of individual artists from whom they are then filtered to the public' (Negus 1997:99). Instead, Peterson argued that 'the nature and content of symbolic products, are shaped by the social, legal and economic milieu in which they are produced' (Peterson 1982:143).

To be able to analyse these milieus Peterson suggested a set of facets 'which alone, or in combination, often constrain or facilitate the evolution of culture' (Peterson 1982:143). The number of facets proposed by Peterson varies between different texts. In a text where Peterson gives a brief presentation of his perspective, five facets are considered to constrain or facilitate the production of popular culture (Peterson 1982). These facets are technology, law, market, organizational structure and occupational careers. In another text (1985), where Peterson analyses the publishing industry, a sixth facet, industry structure, has been added to the previous five. Peterson's understanding of these six facets is briefly discussed below and illuminated by examples taken from the copyright industries.

Technology is used in most kinds of cultural production. If technology changes in some way or another, it will have an implication for the texts being produced. It is easy to identify cases in the history of music production where technology has changed the sound of recorded music: musical instruments, for instance the piano, the electric guitar or the sampler; recording technologies, for instance sophisticated microphones, multi-channel recording or more recently nonlinear recording; distribution technologies, for instance the vinyl disk, the compact cassette, the compact disk or the Internet (e.g. Coleman 2003).

Law – 'Statute law and government regulation shape the financial and aesthetic conditions within which popular culture develops' (Peterson 1982:144). The very term 'copyright' is a legal term, and it is copyright law that transforms cultural expressions into goods that can be traded, bought, sold or infringed.

Industry structure – '. . . the number and relative sizes of the firms in the market producing aesthetic products' (Peterson 1982:144). This facet was indirectly in focus in the Peterson and Berger article from 1975 where they established a relationship between industry structure and cultural diversity (Peterson & Berger 1975).

Organizational structure refers to the structures within the boundaries of the firm, coordinating the activities which generate the cultural products. Sometimes organizational structure and industry structure overlap, for instance due to the development of 'network organizations' (Castells 1996) where the actual boundary of a firm may be difficult to determine.

Occupational careers – '. . . the ways that creative people define their occupations and organize their careers can influence the nature of the work they produce' (Peterson 1982:148). This facet can be illustrated by how the role of the studio engineer

Table 1.1   Levels of aggregation and the facets of the production of culture perspective

Level of aggregation	Related facets
Individual	Occupational career
Organization	Organizational structure
Industry	Market
	Technology
	Law
	Industry structure

has developed parallel to the development of studio recording technologies. In the beginning of the history of recorded music, the studio engineer was very much an engineer who was skilled at handling the equipment in the studio, making sure that the artist's creative ideas were transferred to record as undistorted as possible. Nowadays, the studio engineer is considered to be a musician and sometimes even a star, just like other musicians participating in the recording session (Kealy 1982; Levine & Werde 2003).

The final facet, termed *market*, is a reference to the audience, and specifically how 'financial decision makers redefine the heterogeneous and unknown mass of potential consumers into a homogeneous and predicable "market" that can be tapped through standard market practices' (Peterson 1982:146).

The production of culture perspective is significantly different from the economic and organizational theories previously discussed, not only in terms of its emphasis on cultural products as artefacts rather than commodities but also in its very structure. The production of culture perspective is able to cover all three levels I am interested in this study; individual, organizational and industrial (table 1.1).

Industry dynamics research initiatives typically start with the observation of some kind of change. The change may be new products or genres, changes in consumer behaviour, technology changes, regulatory changes, change in aggregate sales, change in financial performance, change in organizational or industry structures, change in (production/distribution/marketing) routines etc. The purpose of the research initiative is then to gain more knowledge about this change, possibly to be able to understand or explain why the change has occurred or how a change might influence some aspect of the industry. However, the complexity of economic and social systems often makes such attempts very difficult, sometimes even impossible. This is noted by Peterson who considers his production perspective as a 'retreat from confronting the unanswerable questions about the causal links between society and culture' (Peterson 1994:185). Miles and Snow have also reflected on the difficulty of examining these dynamic processes: 'Any attempt to examine organisational adaptation is difficult since the process is both highly complex and changeable' (Miles & Snow 1978:4).

It is important to have the right equipment when engaging in such an apparently arduous exercise. I have gathered our theoretical lenses from the fields of organizational theory, social learning theory and sociology of culture. The frameworks have various intellectual traditions, they complement each other and they share several fundamental qualities. By using these frameworks in concert, I are ready to explore the dynamics of the music industry in the digital age.

2

Inside the Music Industry

This chapter looks *inside* the music industry. I introduce and discuss various definitions of the music industry and try to locate its edges. I identify the three segments of the industry – music recording, music licensing and live music – and present the important characteristics for each sub-industry. This is followed by a brief look in the rear-view mirror, tracing the evolution of the industry during the last century. I will also present some facts and figures of the world's six largest multinational music firms.

What do I mean by the 'music industry'?

An industry is traditionally considered to be a specific part of the economy which is concerned with the factory production of goods aimed for mass consumption. Since the beginning of the industrial revolution the concept of an 'industry' has expanded beyond that traditional definition and now generally is used to refer to the production, marketing and distribution of most commodities, including services and immaterial goods. There are several ways to classify and structure different industrial activities. One of the more common ways is to refer to primary, secondary and tertiary industries, where industries of the first category are, for example, mining and agriculture, industries of the second category are primarily manufacturing and industries of the third category are concerned with service production. Other ways of structuring industries are for instance light vs. heavy industries, business-to-business vs. business-to-consumer industries etc. However, perhaps the most common way to define an industry is to refer to the output from the industrial activity, for instance the travel, automotive or consumer electronics industry. Within any such industry it is also common to structure activities as core activities, supporting activities or related activities.

What then should be considered to be part of the music industry? As with most industries, it is not always perfectly clear what is meant by the term. One definition of the music industry has been suggested by the Swedish Knowledge Foundation (Almqvist & Dahl 2003). In this definition, live music is not considered as a part of the music industry's core. Rather, live music is considered to be a part of the 'performing arts' industry. The core of the music industry is in this definition considered as musicians, songwriters, producers, record companies and music publishers.

In a related, but more elaborated initiative funded by the British government's Department for Culture Media and Sport, the music industry's 'core activities', 'supporting activities' and 'related industries' were defined (DCMS 1998). Yet another definition has been suggested by Engström and Hallencreutz (2003). They did not make a distinction between core and supporting activities, but, like the British government, they defined other industries related to the music industry. Tables 2.1 and 2.2 show there are some differences between them as to how the music industry can be defined. It is of course important to policymakers, trade organizations and others to define the scope and reach of 'their' industries. However, since most copyright industries are evolving, lists such as the ones presented in the tables, usually get outdated relatively quickly.

Negus (1992) approaches the definition issue from a different perspective. He describes the music recording industry as 'concerned with developing global personalities which can be communicated across multiple media; through recordings, videos, films, television, magazines, books and via advertising, product endorsement and sponsorship over a range of consumer merchandise'. In this text, I choose to improve upon Negus's definition, by suggesting two minor adjustments. First, I remove the word 'global' since there are many musical artists that simply are

Table 2.1 The music industry as defined by the British government (DCMS 1998)

Core activities	Supporting activities	Related industries
• Production, distribution and retailing of sound recordings • Administration of copyright in composition and recordings • Live performance (non-classical) • Management, representation and promotion • Songwriting and composition	• Music press • Multimedia content • Digital media • Retailing and distribution of digital music via Internet • Music for computer games • Art and creative studios • Production, distribution and retailing of printed music • Production, retailing and distribution of musical instruments • Jingle production • Photography • Education and training	• Internet/e-commerce • Television and radio • Film and video • Advertising • Performance arts • Interactive leisure software • Software and computer services

Table 2.2 The music industry according to Engström and Hallencreutz (2003:39)

Music industry organizations	Related industries
• Music press • Record labels/producers/studios • Music publishers • Mastering studios • Suppliers of stage equipment • Distributors and wholesalers • Music retailers • Retailers of music instruments and studio equipment • E-business • Management • Artists/musicians/performers • Tour production and concert arrangements • Artist agencies	• Daily press • Other retailers, e.g. gas stations • Hotels • Restaurants, pubs, clubs • Catering • Photography • Graphic design • Video production • Broadcasting • Stylists • Lawyers and auditors

not intended for a global market. Second, I add the words *musical content*, to emphasize the importance of controlling and developing different kinds of intellectual properties. These changes result in the following music industry definition which I will use throughout the text: 'The music industry consists of those companies concerned with developing musical content and personalities which can be communicated across multiple media.'

Three integrated music industries

When trying to stay above the nitty-gritty details of what is or is not part of the music industry, one can generally consider the industry to be constituted of three parts: recording, publishing and live performance (e.g. Hesmondhalgh 2002:12).

Several scholars have tried to explain the logic and dynamics of all these industries, often by presenting various kinds of conceptual industry models.

Leyshon presented one such model (see figure 2.1) which emphasizes that 'the music economy consists of a series of sequential processes' (2001:57). Building on this understanding, Leyshon presents a music industry model primarily based on Attali (1985) and Scott (1999). The model is constituted of four 'musical networks' which 'possess distinctive but overlapping functions, temporalities, and geographies' (Leyshon 2001:60). The first network is one of creativity. The second is a network of reproduction, the third is distribution and the last is a network of consumption. Although Leyshon uses the terms 'network', it is actually only the creativity network that has a 'network-like' structure. The other parts of the model have a relatively linear structure, which means that Leyshon's should be categorized as a fairly traditional value-chain model rather than anything else.

The model begins with the network of creativity where music is created, performed and recorded. This network gravitates around the contractual relationship between the artist and the record company. Leyshon explains this as the core of the music industry where functions such as artists, producers, studio musicians,

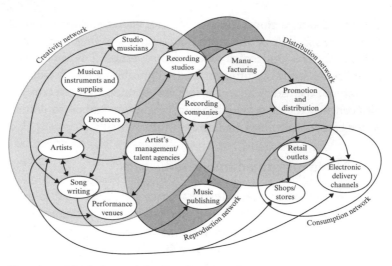

Figure 2.1 Musical networks (Leyshon 2001)

sound engineers, music instruments and supplies, songwriting, artist management, legal services, performance venues, recording studios and recording companies are found (Leyshon 2001). Hence, this understanding of the creative network is based on a wider definition of the music industry than the one I suggest.

Beyond the network of creativity, the networks of reproduction, distribution and consumption are primarily focused on recording and pay less attention to the two other industry sectors.

Being a geographer, Leyshon puts lots of emphasis on the spatial issues of the music industry. Consequently, in the networks termed 'distribution' and 'consumption', where he includes physical promotion, distribution, retail stores and consumers, he is more interested in how the CDs are moved from one place to another than how the music firms are able to raise the consumer's awareness of a certain project. This stands in stark contrast to, for instance, the model introduced by Hirsch (presented later in this chapter) which is focused on the promotion and marketing of music rather than how the physical product is transported from the manufacturing site to the consumers (Leyshon 2001).

Another model which also aims to explain the dynamics of

the music industry which is common to all three sectors is the 'loosely coupled systems model' suggested by Burnett and Weber (1989 – see figure 2.2). 'Loosely coupled' refers to systems in which interactions within subsystems are substantially stronger than interactions between subsystems. (See, for example, Brunner & Brewer 1971; Fisher 1961; Glassman 1973; March & Olsen 1976; Meyer & Rowan 1978; Ouchi 1978; Perrow 1986; Simon 1981; Simon & Ando 1961; Weick 1976). The Burnett and Weber model consists of more or less the same components as Leyshon's model, but the structure is somewhat different. The model is not a linear structure describing how consumer value is created; rather, it shows how different activities or institutions in the industry are related (Burnett & Weber 1989).

The model is structured as two loosely connected systems of production and consumption. The highly complex system for the production of musical culture – the firms, roles, structures and processes – is analytically, if not factually, distinct from the system of cultural consumption. In effect, the connections and ties within these systems are substantially stronger than the connections and ties between them. The relations among record producers, artists, marketing and promotion specialists, trade press and so on are stronger than the relationships between producers and consumers. Consumers of music, once largely the domain of teenagers and young adults, interact among themselves and with mass media, including radio, television and film. Opinion leaders may take into account various fan and music review publications. Weak as these latter ties are, the mainly separate systems of production and consumption are connected through the media, concerts and an economic act: the purchase of music. In the model, the aggregate behaviour of each system is such that it weakly influences the behaviour of the other.

The musical networks model (Leyshon 2001) and the loosely coupled systems model (Burnett & Weber 1989) are both able to point at aspects of the music industry which are common to all three sub-sectors. Next I intend to shift the focus to the specific music industry sub-sectors and examine their distinguishing

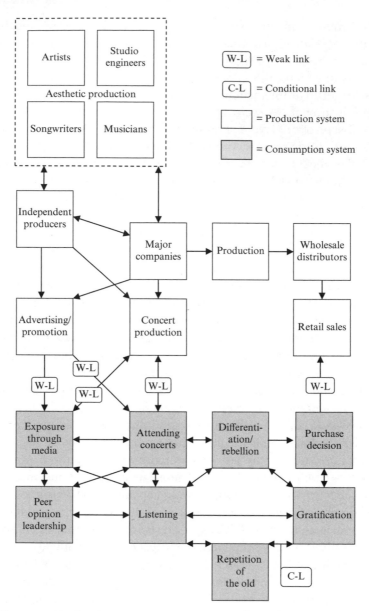

Figure 2.2 Production/consumption systems of popular music
(Burnett & Weber 1989)

ensure the exposure of a particular release. Record companies' promotion of some artists at the expense of others (all under contract to them) is in large part an attempt to structure the ambiguity of this situation' (Hirsch 1970:33).

Promoters and distributors constitute the third subsystem. The function of this subsystem is to filter the output from policy-makers at the record companies. In the scenario described by Hirsch, there are far more record companies than there are promoters. In such a situation, the promoters add value to the process by selecting the songs which they expect to have the best chance of commercial success.

The final subsystem is labelled gatekeepers and is constituted by radio stations and other media outlets. The interdependence between gatekeepers and record companies has already been mentioned in the text. Hirsch adds to the description of this symbiotic relationship by claiming that '. . . radio airplay[16] for a new record is almost always a prerequisite for its sale' (Hirsch 1970:9). However, only very few out of all the albums released are able to get into gatekeepers' playlists. Hirsch continues:

> Radio station managements demand high audience ratings, for the rates charged advertising sponsors (i.e. the station's income) are based solely on the number of listeners the station can 'deliver'. Advertising agencies place ads with radio stations according to the 'cost per thousand' listeners. The fierce competition between stations requires that the program director successfully select a group of records that will appeal to the widest possible audience. (Hirsch 1970:61)

Consequently, 'the record promoter [. . .] must operate within the context of the station programmer's quest for certainty. The programme director is constantly on the lookout for advance intelligence regarding the "hit" potential of every record he selects for airplay' (Hirsch 1970:56). The record promoter tries to address this request by providing sales figures to demonstrate his records' popularity.

Hirsch's model was the fruition of one of the first attempts to explore the music industry. A reasonable question is whether the

features. I start out with the sector which dominated the music industry during the twentieth century – music recording.

Recording

The record company's traditional business model involves the production of intellectual properties by recording artists' studio or live performances. The record company then markets and distributes these recordings to consumers around the world.

The sociologist Paul Hirsch was one of the first scholars to analyse the recording industry in a serious manner. In 1970 he presented a model which aimed to explain how music becomes popular. Hirsch's model describes that part of the recording industry which traditionally is referred to as the 'top 40 music industry'. The top 40 format was invented in the US during the 1950s when the new television medium forced the radio medium to change its programming (e.g. Thorburn & Jenkins 2003). A radio station which follows this format plays the 40 most popular songs during a certain week. 'Most popular' is in this case equal to the records which have sold the most during the week. Still to this day, similar formats are used by most commercial mainstream radio stations. 'Top 40' is today referred to as contemporary hit radio (CHR) and is but one of many different radio formats. Other formats are for instance classic rock, country, urban, adult contemporary (AC), news/talk, oldies, modern rock, classical and smooth jazz.

The record labels which are producing music aimed for the 'top 40 music industry' are heavily dependent on the commercial radio stations for the promotion of their artists and music. Hirsch recognized the close relationship between the two copyright industries: 'The record and radio industry have grown up together and live in a symbiotic relationship. Each plays an important role in the dissemination and popularization of culture; both have affected its form and its direction. Although mutually dependent organizations, their goals vary, and oftimes conflict' (Hirsch 1970:10). This relationship is clearly illustrated by figure 2.3 where the 'pop music industry' is mapped to the preselection system framework.[15]

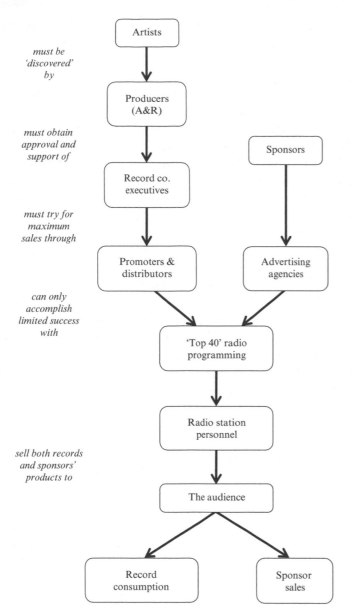

must be
'discovered'
_by_

must obtain
approval and
support of

must try for
maximum
sales through

can only
accomplish
limited success
with

sell both records
and sponsors'
products to

Figure 2.3 The organization of the recording industry (Hirsch 1970:17A)

A great amount of 'filtering' takes place at each of the stages of the preselection system. It is only a small fraction of all artists that ever are able to even meet an A&R (artist and repertoire) agent, and only very few out of all the acts that an A&R agent ever listens to get the attention of the record executive etc. Eventually only one artist 'in a million' will be heard by the mainstream audience on commercial radio stations.

Hirsch has identified four subsystems within the music industry, which the artist has to pass through to be able to reach the final subsystem, the audience. Below, Hirsch's understanding of these four subsystems will be briefly presented.

The first subsystem is the creative sector, including the artist, the producer and the A&R agent. Hirsch states that 'the success of every performing artist is closely tied to the number of his records that come to the attention of and are purchased by the public. Records are the means by which an artist gains or enlarges his popular following' (Hirsch 1970:25). The A&R agent is the first strategic checkpoint in the preselection process which eventually may take the artist all the way to commercial success. The agents have a crucial job since they are the ones who will find new talents with artistic as well as commercial potential. It is critical to each record company to continuously find new talents since the life of a 'hit' record is only from 60 to 120 days. 'Replacements are needed for those items currently on the "charts". The unknown artist and the companies each share a vital interest in his discovery and success, for the hit record industry is based on the fads of the moment. The styles in vogue change rapidly and unpredictably' (Hirsch 1970:25).

The second subsystem is the record company. When an artist has been discovered by an A&R agent, the next step is to meet the record company policy-makers. These men and women have the task of selecting from the output of the creative subsystem the records which are to be released (Hirsch 1970:31). Hirsch notes that 'while the decision to release a record is theirs, policymakers have little control over the media, little power to model has any relevance almost four decades after it was developed. Through the years, the model has been criticized but it still is able to encapsulate important aspects of the workings of the mainstream recording industry. For instance, there still are gatekeepers in the new music economy even though they look very different from those of the 1970s. Music still has to be exposed to the audience in order for listeners to be able to determine its value. Broadcast radio is to some extent losing its importance, but is replaced by other types of media. Advertisers or sponsors are probably even more important to the music industry today than they were forty years ago.

Publishing

While the recording industry is a business-to-consumer industry, the music publishing segment of the music industry has nowadays almost no direct contact with the music audience. Composers and lyricists engage a publisher to license their works for various purposes, such as traditional recordings, sheet music, live performances or background music in video productions. The royalties paid by the licensee flow via various mechanisms to the composer or lyricist as one of three different royalty categories. *Performance* royalties are paid when a song is performed by an orchestra or singer, played by a radio station, used as a mobile phone ringtone, played in a shopping mall etc. *Synchronization* royalties are paid when a song is used together with moving images, for instance a movie or a videogame. *Mechanical* royalties are paid based on actual sales of sheet music and audio recordings (e.g. Vogel 2001:157–8).

Traditionally, music publishing royalties are split fifty/fifty, with half going to the publisher as payment for their services and the rest going to the composers and lyricists. Some music publishers also fill other business roles, with regard to writers and artists – many serve as record producers, and vice versa, or as artist managers. This is generally considered acceptable, although sometimes aspects of one role can negatively impact on other dealings a publisher or manager may have with their client.

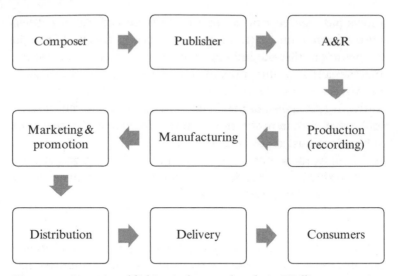

Figure 2.4 A music publishing industry value chain (Wallis 2004:105)

Figure 2.4 shows a music industry value chain, with a specific focus on music publishing and the licensing of songs to record companies. The model explains how the composer creates the work and normally signs an agreement with a publisher. In Wallis's value chain, the only possibility is to have the song picked up by a record company's A&R department and subsequently recorded by an artist. There are of course other opportunities and revenue sources available to the composer. These are recognized by Wallis, but left out of the graphical representation (Wallis 2004).

Live performance
Although the size of the recorded music industry is bigger than the live music industry, from the artists' point of view, live music generally is a more important source of income than recorded music. Since most pop music performers do not achieve success in the recording industry, most of them have to make a living as musicians in pubs, clubs and other similar venues. As a consequence, out of all musicians and composers active in the

music industry, most of them are primarily working in the live performance segment. In addition, artists generally receive up to 85 per cent of the gross revenues from a live music project while they usually receive approximately 10 per cent from recorded music revenues.

The live music segment of the music industry is a multifaceted and complex system. Live music is performed in busy streets and subway stations, at private parties, at local pubs, rock festivals, at clubs, at sports arenas and amphitheatres. The concerts can be one-off shows, tours or a series of shows at a single venue. These characteristics of the industry make it very difficult to measure and analyse. It is difficult to delineate the industry and to gather data, for instance, for all the smaller gigs played at pubs and private parties around the world. The part of the industry which often gets most attention is for obvious reasons the one with the largest and most spectacular global tours with the brightest shining superstars. However, this part of the industry is not only important due to its glamour; the live music industry is very top-heavy in the sense that a small number of large projects constitute a large percentage of the total industry. The 'top-heaviness' of the industry adds to the measurement difficulties. The size of the industry varies greatly between different years depending on which artists decide to go on tour that particular year.

Besides the performer, there are three other important actors operating in the live music industry, namely the booking agent, the promoter and the venue operator. The booking agent works on behalf of the artist and contracts the promoter to arrange the events. Booking agents usually get a fixed fee or a percentage fee from the performer, and the promoters earn their revenue primarily from the sales of tickets. The performers are paid by the promoters according to a formula which may differ between artists and between events. The formula usually includes a guaranteed payment and a percentage of ticket sales or event revenues. The performer may be reimbursed for various production costs such as sound or lights. Promoters, together with the performers, managers and booking agents jointly determine the price of the tickets, an important issue to which I will return later in this section. The promoters normally market the events, sell tickets, make agreements with local venue operators etc. The venue operators normally provide additional services such as parking, security, ticket-collecting etc. The venue operators typically receive percentages of the ticket sales as well as of concession sales and merchandise sales.

The North American as well as the European live music industry today is dominated by Live Nation, a publicly listed company which was spun off from Clear Channel Communications in 2005. Live Nation is a vertically integrated company, which has booking rights for, or equity stakes in, 155 venues around the world including the Fillmore in San Francisco and Wembley arena in London. Besides being one of the world's largest venue operators, they are the world's leading promoter and were during 2007 involved in 28,000 events and sold more than 45 million tickets to various live music events. In 2007 the company's live music business areas generated $3.1 billion in revenues. As with the difficulties in accurately measuring the size of the live music industry, it is also difficult to accurately determine Live Nation's market share, but, generally, it is assumed that the company's share of the market is considerably more than 50 per cent.

Although considerably outdistanced by Live Nation, the second largest actor in the live music industry is AEG Live, a subsidiary of Anschutz Entertainment Group. AEG Live has during the past few years expanded its live music business and is slowly establishing itself as the global number two. Beyond these two multinationals, the live music industry is very fragmented and primarily consists of national or regional players.

A brief history of the music recording industry

In order to understand the music industry in the digital age, it is important to know where the industry is coming from. The history of music may be traced back to the Upper Palaeolithic age, and sometimes even further back, but the historical account I aim for in this section will have a somewhat shorter scope. The historical narrative will follow the evolution of the *industrial* aspects of music culture, and especially those aspects which are related to music recording. There are several accounts of the history of the international recording industry, (e.g. Barfe 2004; Coleman 2003; Gelatt 1977; Gronow 1983; Gronow & Saunio 1998; Qualen 1985; Read & Welch 1976). This section is primarily based on these sources.

The history of the music recording industry can be described in many ways. One is to focus on how different genres have evolved and been rejected or embraced by the business and the audience. Another is to use technological milestones as the framework for laying out the industry's evolution and to follow how formats for distribution, listening devices or production technologies and musical instruments have developed. This is the perspective I will start out with in this account, but I will also try to combine the technological perspective with a focus on the major firms of the recording industry. Primarily I will focus on how firms have been established and discontinued, and how firms have acquired or merged with each other.

Music has been the basis of viable businesses for centuries, but, through the ages, the balance between the three segments of recording, publishing and live performance has fluctuated. Before the advent of print technology, the music industry consisted of only one of the three segments, namely the live performance business. Obviously, it is somewhat anachronistic to ascribe terms such as 'industry' to the work of musicians of this age. The activities of musicians outside the churches, monasteries and royal courts were not very industrial in their character, but at least the musicians were able to make a living through their trade. As print technology evolved, sheet music slowly became a second product which could be sold to the growing European urban middle classes. Music fans at the end of the nineteenth and beginning of the twentieth century, who wanted to listen to music, most likely had to play the music themselves.

They learned about music from friends, or by listening to performers at the local bandstands and vaudevilles. When they
heard a song that they liked, those who could afford it bought the
sheet music at the local stationery store and played the popular
piece on the piano in their living room. One of the most successful works during the turn of the twentieth century was 'After the
Ball', by Charles Harris, which was popularized at the Chicago
World's Fair, and sold over two million sheet-music copies. In
1907, another song, 'School Days', by Gus Edwards, sold over
three million copies.

The centre of gravity in the industry which produced the sheet
music was located on 28th Street between Broadway and Sixth
Avenue in New York City. In this area, often referred to as 'Tin
Pan Alley',[17] offices of music publishing companies were packed
wall to wall. In some rooms, songwriters wrote tunes at a piano,
and in another room lyricists were trying to come up with new
catchy phrases. Tin Pan Alley came to represent the entire pop
music industry of its day. Tin Pan Alley publishers produced
songs and promoted them as commodities. The publishers had
composers contracted who wrote songs to reflect the current
topics and to imitate the latest hits. Publishers used different
techniques to promote and market the songs, with vaudevillians
playing a major role in their efforts. Music publishers aggressively marketed their products to vaudeville performers in a
number of ways, for instance via ads in the trade newspaper and
via 'song-pluggers' who tried to persuade variety performers to
pick up the new songs (e.g. Barfe 2004; Poe 1997).

The new sound-recording technologies developed during the
end of the nineteenth century, primarily by Edison, Columbia
and Victor, challenged the incumbent industry structure and
changed the core product of the music industry from printed sheet
music to shellac discs. Initially, these three companies considered
musical content as merely a means for promoting the sales of
gramophones, but during the 1920s the focus was more and more
turned towards the musical content and away from the hardware.

These three firms more or less defined the role of the 'record company'. They chose to include the task of finding and developing new musical personalities, as well as the manufacturing, marketing and distribution of the physical products as parts of their businesses. The music publishers which previously had been such important actors in the music industry were reduced to administering copyrights of composers and lyricists and to collecting royalties from the sales of records and other kinds of music licensing.

During the 1930s and 1940s the music industry continued to be moulded by societal and technological developments. The three original major music firms evolved through mergers, bankruptcies and acquisitions into a new trio: RCA/Victor, EMI and CBS Records. These three companies came to dominate the international music industry during the following decades and they still constitute the core of the world's two largest music firms (EMI and Sony Music). A few new record companies (e.g. Decca, Mercury and Capitol) joined the trio during this period, but the music industry structure largely continued to be characterized by a high level of concentration.

At the end of the 1950s and during the 1960s the consolidated structure of the music industry was shaken to its foundations. The development is usually explained by referring to the advent of rock 'n' roll music in concert with changes in the broadcast media environment. First, although the major firms successfully signed a number of significant rock 'n' roll acts, the new genre enabled smaller innovative firms to become at least temporarily commercially successful at the expense of the major firms. Second, in broadcast media, the growth of the television medium forced radio stations to revise their programming. In order to face the competition from the new medium, the radio turned to music in order to get access to popular content for free or at a low price.

One important consequence of the evolution of the broadcast media was the establishment of the radio medium as the music firms' most important promotional tool. By exposing their music in the broadcast media, they encouraged a portion of the audience to purchase the same music in the record stores.

This straightforward business model, which was established in the mid-1950s, prevailed for several decades, and it was not challenged until the coming of Internet-based music distribution technologies at the very end of the last century.

The 1990s saw the development of digital technology which led to the unprecedented growth of the recording industry, leading to its peak in worldwide music sales in 1998 (figure 2.5). This expansion is primarily linked to the advent of the CD in 1982, which until recently was the dominant music format. The boost to music sales was significant as the introduction of the more durable CD format led many music consumers to replace their LP collections with CDs. It can be argued that this replacement effect and corresponding sales increases created by CDs was an unusual one which will be difficult to initiate on new formats. Indeed newer formats like digital audio tapes (DAT), digital compact cassettes (DCC) and minidisks (MD) were not commercial successes. Often this lack of uptake of new formats has also been the result of differences among different groups of hardware and software companies, who have promoted incompatible formats.

The new century saw the decline of CD sales and the rise of digital technology and the widespread use of the Internet in particular. To date, the mix of digital technology and the Internet has proven to be more of a challenge than an opportunity to the music industry. First, the huge increase of online music piracy has been identified by the music industry as one of the main reasons for the drop in sales revenues since 1999. It is of course extremely difficult to establish a causal link between online piracy and declining industry sales. What is clear is that unauthorized file-sharing over peer-to-peer (P2P) networks that do not remunerate artists, composers, producers and rights holders, while potentially violating copyright laws, have thrown into question the very existence of the traditional music business model.

The overall effects of rising cost bases, the decline in sales and profit margins and the restructuring of the entertainment companies that own the major music companies have resulted

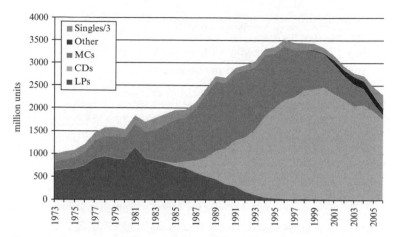

Notes: It is common IFPI practice to split singles sales numbers by three in order to make them more comparable to full-length albums. 'Other' formats include music videos (DVD, VHS etc.) as well as SACD, MiniDisk, etc. Digital singles are included in singles sales from 2004.

Figure 2.5 Global music sales by format (IFPI 2007)

in cost-cutting, industry-wide layoffs, consolidation, shrinking budgets for development of new acts and significant cuts in artist rosters. It is estimated that the four majors have each shed over 25 per cent of the workforce since the turn of the century. During the same period they have cut their artist rosters also by more than 25 per cent.

As this brief account of the history of the music industry shows, the industry is intrinsically connected to the development of technologies for recording and disseminating music. Various technologies have been developed for that purpose, and figure 2.6. lists some of the more important milestones in this evolution.

The relationship between majors and indies

The developments presented in the previous section have cultivated an industry structure characterized by a small number of

1877	Edison demonstrates cylinder phonograph.
1887	Emile Berliner granted patent for disk gramophone.
1906	Victor introduces the Victrola, the first successful mass-market phonograph.
1925	The Victor Company releases the first commercial electrical recording.
1948	Columbia introduces the 33 RPM record.
1949	RCA introduces the 45 RPM record.
1958	Audio Fidelity releases the first commercial stereo record.
1964	Philips presents the Compact Cassette tape (CC) format.
1979	Sony offers a personal tape player called the Soundabout, the first Walkman.
1982	Sony and Philips introduce the compact disk (CD) format.
1989	MP3 compression technology patented by Fraunhofer Institute in Erlangen, Germany.
1993	IUMA (Internet Underground Music Archive) opens.
1998	Portable MP3 players developed by Diamond Multimedia and SaeHan Information Systems.
1999	Shawn Fanning launched the first popularized file-sharing peer-to-peer network.
2001	Rhapsody launches first flat-fee, all-you-can-eat, music subscription service.
2001	Apple launches the iPod.
2003	Apple launches the iTunes Music Store.
2007	Streamed and on-demand music becomes part of the Billboard Hot 100 chart formula.

Figure 2.6 Milestones in music technology development

multinational music companies controlling a substantial part of the global music-related sales.

Traditionally, a distinguishing characteristic of these major music companies was that they controlled considerable resources for manufacturing and distribution of the physical product. As has previously been discussed, these dominating record companies have traditionally been referred to as majors while all other record companies were referred to as independents. In the digital age, when resources for manufacturing and physical distribution have lost most of their significance, the terms major and independents have remained, primarily to distinguish the four largest music companies from all the other ones. However, the terms are far from clear and undisputed. For instance, EMI Group has often referred to itself as the 'world's largest independent music company' (e.g. EMI 2008)!

The links between indies and majors have always been strong. Since indies often accept a higher level of risk than the larger companies, they have been able to develop new genres, sounds and artists which have not fitted into the majors' mainstream thinking. When an artist who is signed to an indie label has grown to a certain level, it is common that a major acquires either the artist's contract or the entire label, in order to get access to the talent and to take it to the next level. (The relationship between indies and majors is also discussed in chapter 4.)

During the last six decades, the majors have developed the practice of acquiring talents from smaller labels into a well-established innovation strategy. Major record labels in the beginning of the 1950s primarily had a monolithic and hierarchical organizational structure which had been common practice since the earliest days of the industry. Most of the crucial decisions regarding the development of new talents and products were concentrated in a group of men at the top of the organization. These decision-makers were prone to promote their own established talents rather than to look for new talents and new forms of expression.

Due to this proclivity for the old, the majors initially were very hesitant about the new sounds of rock 'n' roll and rhythm 'n' blues during the 1950s and were convinced that the fads would soon blow over. As time progressed they slowly started to realize that the sounds were there to stay. One of the first signs of the majors' change of mind, and also one of the largest acquisitions during the period, was RCA's acquisition of the Elvis Presley contract from Sun Records in 1953 for $35,000. While all the other majors were unable to stay in the charts during the 1950s, this single acquisition enabled RCA to remain.

The 1950s and 1960s taught the majors a lesson of how not to deal with changes in the audience's preferences. To address the problem, many major record companies changed their relationship with the smaller labels. Rather than considering the indies as threats and something that should be driven out of business as quickly as possible, the majors began to build business relationships with them. The majors realized that the indies were able to find new artists and genres much more efficiently than they could themselves. By then signing so-called 'upstream' deals with the indies, the majors had the option of acquiring contracts with promising talents, or of entering into partial ownership with the label, or sometimes even acquiring the label altogether.

The relationship between the indies and the majors continued to evolve during the 1970s. When a small label was acquired by a larger one, it was not dissolved within the acquirer's organization as in the old days. Rather, the acquired firm was given a considerable level of freedom and was able to continue its operations almost as before the acquisition. One example of such an acquisition and innovation strategy is the formation of Warner Records. During the 1970s and the beginning of the 1980s, Kinney (Warner Communications) made deals with close to thirty record labels, either through acquisitions or through alliances, and created a loosely held recording powerhouse where the creative decision-making to a great extent was decentralized. As long as the sub-labels delivered the expected financial results, they were more or less allowed to make their own decisions concerning the label's artist portfolio. 'The Warner model' enabled the majors to quickly adapt to changes in the audience's preferences. As an evidence of the model's capability, since the 1960s, new genres such as disco, metal, grunge, rap, hip-hop etc. have all been quickly picked up by the majors and turned into profitable styles.

During the 1990s, the upstreaming strategy was developed a step further. When the strategy was introduced in the 1950s and 1960s, the majors still continued to scout unsigned talents which over a number of years could be developed into major talents and profitable products. Since then, such scouting activities have been radically reduced, and now almost the entire talent-development capability of the recording industry resides within the smaller record companies. The majors await the development of the talents signed by the indies and offer upstream deals to those talents that seem to be ready to be taken to the next level. The other internal change at the major record companies relates to the level of centralization of the creative decision-making. Due to the shrinking size of record sales, the majors have tried to reduce costs by grouping their labels into label groups which share and coordinate different resources and processes. Some of the groups still allow the internal labels a considerable degree of freedom while other groups are more or less a single organizational entity which runs the labels as a number of brands or product categories. As a result, rather than having a large number of labels (thirty-plus) within the organization which compete against each other, most majors now have only a handful of well-coordinated label groups. Whether this structure is still able to cope with the rapidly changing preferences of audiences or whether the record companies will again end up in the same situation as during the 1950s remains to be seen.

The current size and structure of the international market

It is fairly difficult to measure accurately individual music companies' share of national or global sales. However, on a global level, the four largest firms control approximately 72 per cent of the music-recording market. The value is somewhat higher in North America and Europe, and somewhat lower in Asia (EMI 2007; IFPI 2004b; Vivendi 2007; Warner Music 2007).

In 2008, the global trade value of recorded music sales was approximately $18 billion, which is only 50 per cent of the value in 1999 (IFPI 2009). The global music market has during the last decade been concentrated to five giants: (from largest in size to smallest) the US, Japan, the United Kingdom, Germany and France. Combined, these five territories constitute approximately three-quarters of the global market. The US is by far the largest within the group with a trade value during 2008 of $5.0 billion. It is interesting to relate the size of the US market to the sizes of the European ($7.3 billion) and Asian markets. These three markets (the US, Europe, Asia) constitute 93 per cent of the global market. The rest of the world accounts for the remaining per cent of sales. It is important to observe that some markets may be large and

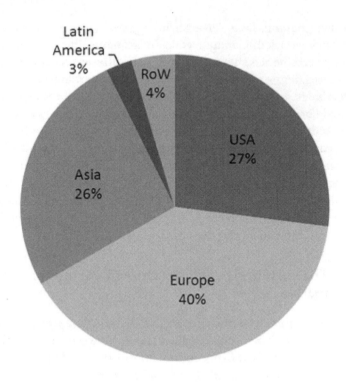

Source: IFPI 2009

Figure 2.7 Recorded music sales 2008 (trade values, US$ millions).

important music markets but it may, for various reasons, be difficult to get useful data for these areas. One such market is China where it is estimated that 90 per cent of all recorded music sold is illegal.

Even if the international market to a great extent is controlled by the four majors, it is important to note that the music market, as most other media markets, is not a single coherent worldwide market. Rather it is structured as a large number of distinct local markets, and music firms have to adapt their content to the local taste of each market (e.g. Aris & Bughin 2005). Although the majors certainly have the capacity to develop and maintain worldwide brands of selected artists, domestic artists without an international following are also of considerable importance to their businesses. In 2006, the domestic music repertoire accounted for 44 per cent of an average country's total recorded music sales, and on a worldwide aggregated level, more than two-thirds of the global recorded music sales were generated from domestic music repertoire (IFPI 2007). Domestic music is of considerable importance to the industry, but the specific level of importance varies both in space and in time. First, the percentage of total sales constituted by domestic music ('domestic music share') varies considerably between different countries (table 2.3). In some countries the value is less than 10 per cent, while in others it is more than 90 per cent (IFPI 2007). Second, global sales of recorded music declined by approximately 18 per cent between 1999 and 2006, but sales of international repertoire lost 28 per cent while the corresponding value for domestic repertoire was less than 13 per cent (ibid.). Whatever might be the causes of the general decline, it seems as if music created by domestic artists is more resilient to those causes than music created by artists from countries far away (Picard & Wikström 2008).

Presentation of the world's largest music companies

The dominant multinational music companies are extremely important in the development of most aspects of the music industry. I will in the final section of this chapter give a brief presentation of the major companies in recorded music, music publishing and live music.

In total, six companies will be presented. Obviously, I will include the four companies usually categorized as the majors (Universal Music Group, Sony Music Entertainment, EMI Group and Warner Music Group), but I will also include relevant data from Sony/ATV Music Publishing and Live Nation, which are operating in the music-publishing sector and the live music

Table 2.3 The domestic music share of the world's forty-two largest music markets

Country	DMS[18]	Country	DMS
New Zealand	9%	Spain	41%
Switzerland	10%	Hong Kong	42%
Austria	12%	Argentina	43%
Belgium	17%	Germany	45%
Chile	20%	Italy	46%
Malaysia	20%	Mexico	46%
Canada	21%	Finland	47%
Netherlands	21%	UK	50%
Ireland	23%	Czech Rep.	52%
Singapore	25%	Taiwan	55%
Portugal	25%	Greece	57%
Australia	26%	France	57%
Norway	27%	Indonesia	58%
Colombia	29%	South Korea	61%
South Africa	32%	Russia	69%
Sweden	35%	Thailand	70%
Poland	35%	Brazil	71%
Philippines	37%	Japan	75%
Denmark	39%	Turkey	87%
Hungary	39%	India	90%
China	40%	US	93%

sector respectively. Each company will be described through a short background, a panel with some current data and, when relevant, a graph illustrating the major mergers and acquisitions that have resulted in their current organizational structure.

Universal Music Group

Universal Music Group (UMG) is the world's largest record company, controlling around 26 per cent of the official global music market (IFPI 2007). UMG is part of the French media conglomerate Vivendi, but is headquartered in New York City, USA.

UMG has two main business areas: publishing and recorded music. The organization has evolved over the decades through large and small mergers and acquisitions, as illustrated by figure 2.8. Through the 2007 acquisition of the music publishing entity from the German media conglomerate Bertelsmann, UMG established itself not only as the world's largest record company but also as the world's largest music publisher. UMG was profitable during 2007, with an operating income of €624 million and revenues amounting to €4.9 billion.

The panel below lists some of the current data on Universal Music Group. Do note that this information is often changed; visit http://www.musicinthecloud.net for updated information. The history of Universal Music, visualized as a series of acquisitions and mergers, is illustrated by figure 2.8

UNIVERSAL MUSIC GROUP

Company: Universal Music Group (record company and music publisher)
Headquarters: Santa Monica and New York City, US
Global presence: Offices in seventy-one countries
Parent company: Vivendi (France) 100%
Management: Douglas Morris (Chairman and CEO)
Employees worldwide: 7915
Revenues (2007): €4.9 billion (music publishing: €589 million)
Operating income (2007): €624 million
Global market position – recorded music: #1 (Market share 26%)
Global market position – music publishing: #1 (Market share 22%)
Controls record labels such as: A&M, Decca, Geffen, Interscope, Island, Def Jam, Lost Highway, Machete, Mercury, Motown and Verve
Represents artists and songwriters such as: 50 Cent, Al Jarreau, Amy Winehouse, B. B. King, Beck, Berliner Philharmoniker, Bjork (Outside US and UK), Bon Jovi, Bryan Adams, Def Leppard, Diana Krall, Diana Ross, Elton John, Elvis Costello, Gwen Stefani, Guns N' Roses, Herbie Hancock, India Arie, Kanye West, Kiss, Limp Bizkit, Linkin Park, Ludacris, Macy Gray, Mariah Carey, Marilyn Manson, Mary J. Blige, Metallica (outside US), Morrissey, Nelly Furtado, PJ Harvey, Robert Plant, Shania Twain, Snow Patrol, Sting, The Hives and U2

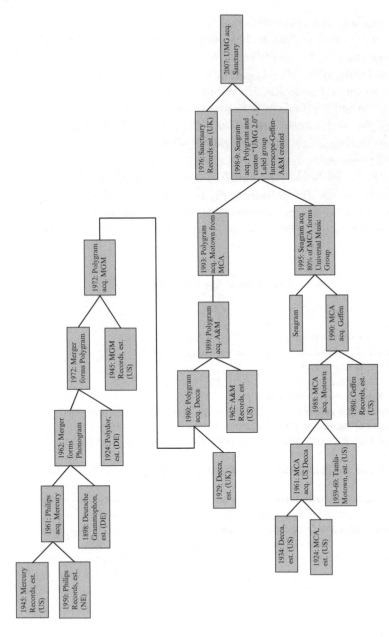

Figure 2.8 Noteworthy mergers and acquisitions during the development of Universal Music Group

Sony Music Entertainment

Sony Music Entertainment is the world's second-largest music company, holding approximately 25 per cent of the official global music market (IFPI 2007). The company was formed as a 50/50 merger (called Sony BMG) in 2004, between Sony Music Entertainment and Bertelsmann's music division, BMG. In October 2008, Sony Corporation acquired Bertelsmann's 50 per cent in the company and changed the name back to Sony Music Entertainment.

Sony Music Entertainment was established when Sony acquired CBS at the end of 1987 as a strategic move into the world of content. The consumer electronics industry and the entertainment industry have always been very close, and by controlling assets in both industries Sony hopes, among other things, to be able to control the development of new information-storage formats. Over the years, Sony has had both good and bad experiences of format battles, including the Betamax failure and the success of the Compact Disc. Sony has also tried to

---

SONY MUSIC ENTERTAINMENT

Company: Sony Music Entertainment (record company)
Headquarters: New York City, US
Global presence: Offices in forty-six countries
Global market position (recorded music): #2 (Market share 20%)
Parent company: Sony Corporation (Japan)
Management: Rolf Schmidt-Holz (CEO)
Employees worldwide: Approximately 3000
Revenues (2007): €3 billion
Controls record labels such as: Arista, Bluebird Jazz, BNA, Burgundy, Columbia, Epic, J Records, Jive, LaFace Legacy, Masterworks, Provident, RCA, RCA Victor, Windham Hill and Zomba
Represents artists such as: Celine Dion, Bob Dylan, Foo Fighters, Kenny G, Alicia Keys, Avril Lavigne, Leona Lewis, Sarah McLachlan, Elvis Presley, Eros Ramazzotti, Santana, Shakira, Frank Sinatra, Bruce Springsteen, Rod Stewart and Justin Timberlake

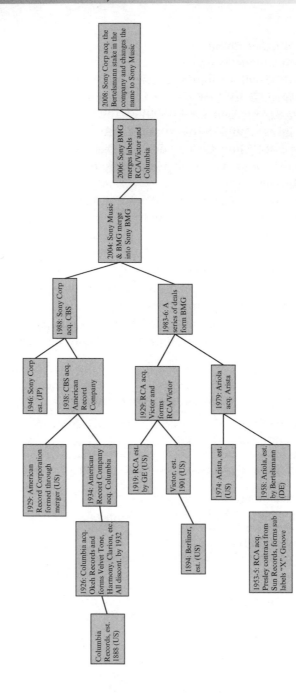

Figure 2.9 Noteworthy mergers and acquisitions during the development of Sony Music

launch several other physical carriers and formats such as DAT, Minidisc, UMD and Blue Ray.

The panel above lists some of the current data on Sony Music Entertainment. Do note that this information is often changed; visit http://www.musicinthecloud.net for updated information. The history of Sony Music, visualized as a series of acquisitions and mergers, is illustrated by figure 2.9.

Warner Music Group

The Warner Music Group (WMG) was formed in 2004 when Time Warner liquidated corporate assets and sold the Warner Music division (record labels and publishing division) to a private investment group led by Edgar Bronfman Jr. Warner Music is now the world's third-largest music conglomerate, holding

---

WARNER MUSIC GROUP

Company: Warner Music Group (record company and music publisher)
Headquarters: New York City, US
Global presence: Offices in forty-one countries
Parent company: Publicly traded at the New York Stock Exchange
Management: Edgar Bronfman, Jr (Chairman and CEO)
Revenues (2008): $3.5 billion (music publishing: $600 million (approx.))
Operating income (2008): $207 million (music publishing: $58 million(approx.))
Employees worldwide: Approx. 3800
Global market position – recorded music: #3 (market share 14%)
Global market position – music publishing: #3 (market share 15%)
Controls record labels such as: Asylum, Atlantic, Bad Boy Cordless, East West, Elektra, Lava Maverick, Nonesuch, Reprise, Rhino, Sire, Warner Bros, Word
Represents artists and songwriters such as: Eric Clapton, Green Day, Dr. Dre, Faith Hill, George and Ira Gershwin, Nickelback, Morrissey, Madonna, Laura Pausini, Red Hot Chili Peppers, Cole Porter, Rob Thomas and Led Zeppelin

approximately 15 per cent of the official global music market (IFPI 2007). WMG has, since the Bronfman acquisition, been through a difficult restructuring process in which 30 per cent of their artist roster has been cut, and those artists who do not sell enough have been dropped. They have also terminated contracts with megastars such as Madonna, who had been with them for her entire career. However, some early signs may indicate that Bronfman is doing something right. Between 2004 and 2008, the sales of recorded music from the other three major music companies declined by percentages with two-digit numbers, while Warner Music Group were actually able to increase their sales by 5 per cent (Lowry 2008). Whether this is a temporary fluke or a sign of long-term skilful management it is too early to say, but it is enough reason to keep an eye on Warner Music Group.

The panel above lists some of the current data on Warner Music. Do note that this information is often changed; visit http://www.musicinthecloud.net for updated information. The history of Warner Music, visualized as a series of acquisitions and mergers, is illustrated by figure 2.10.

EMI Group
EMI was purchased in 2007 by the private equity firm Terra Firma. After assuming control of the company, Terra Firma delisted the EMI Group's shares from the London Stock Exchange, which led to mass speculation as to the future of the music company. Terra Firma started a massive restructuring of EMI which included firing senior staff and selling off numerous corporate assets. During the restructuring process, EMI has had serious difficulty keeping some of its most valuable artist contracts. For instance, Radiohead, The Rolling Stones and Paul McCartney have all left due to the demands of cooperating with the new EMI management (Parrack 2008). EMI is not yet free from their hardship and it remains to be seen how the company will develop in the future. For many years, EMI and Warner Music Group have been close to a merger, or to an acquisition by

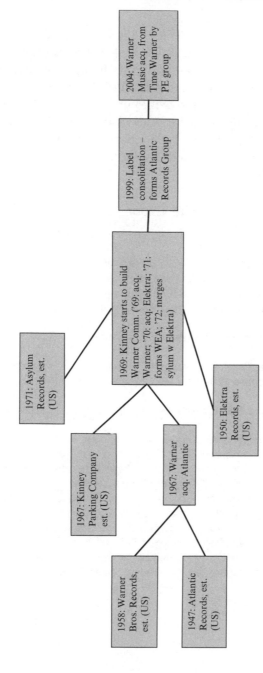

Figure 2.10 Noteworthy mergers and acquisitions during the development of Warner Music Group

one of the other, and that still looks like a possible development. Although EMI is a troubled music major, it is still the world's fourth-largest music company and controls approximately 13 per cent of the official global music market (IFPI 2007).

The panel below lists some of the current data on EMI Group. Do note that this information is often changed; visit http://www. musicinthecloud.net for updated information. The history of EMI Group, visualized as a series of acquisitions and mergers, is illustrated by figure 2.11.

EMI GROUP

Company: EMI Group (music publisher and record company)
Headquarters: London, UK
Global presence: Offices in fifty countries.
Parent company: Terra Firma Capital Partners
Management: Elio Leoni-Sceti (CEO)
Global market position – recorded music: #4 (Market share: 11%)
Global market position – music publishing: #2 (Market share: 20%)
Revenues (2007): £1.5 billion (music publishing £411 million)
Operating income (2007): £164 million (music publishing £116 million)
Controls record labels such as: Angel, Blue Note, Capitol, Mute, Parlophone, Virgin etc.
Represents artists and songwriters such as: ABBA, Alicia Keys, Anita Baker, Arctic Monkeys, Blur, Cliff Richard, Coldplay, Count Basie, Daft Punk, Dandy Warhols, David Bowie, Depeche Mode, Duran Duran, Earth Wind & Fire, Ed Harcourt, Fats Domino, Gorillaz, Iggy Pop, Iron Maiden, James Blunt, Janet Jackson, John Lennon, Judas Priest, Kanye West, Kate Bush, Kraftwerk, Kylie, Lenny Kravitz, Louis Armstrong, Massive Attack, Miles Davis, Moby, Natasha Bedingfield, Nirvana, Norah Jones, Pet Shop Boys, Pharrell Williams, Phil Collins, Pink Floyd, Queen, Richard Ashcroft, Rod Stewart, Sarah Brightman, Stevie Wonder, Sting, The Beach Boys, The Beatles, The Prodigy, Usher and White Stripes

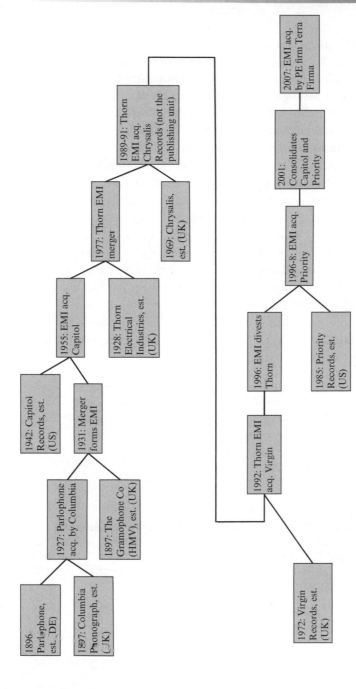

Figure 2.11 Noteworthy mergers and acquisitions during the development of EMI Group

Sony/ATV Music Publishing

Sony/ATV Publishing is today the world's largest stand-alone music-publishing company. It was formed in 1995 through the merger between ATV Music, which Michael Jackson had acquired in 1985, and Sony's publishing arm. One of the most valuable possessions in the Sony/ATV catalogue is the Northern Songs catalogue which mainly consists of 180 songs written by the Beatles. The Beatles members had formed Northern Songs together with their publisher Dick James and their manager Brian Epstein in 1963. In a series of unfortunate events, the Beatles lost control of Northern Songs when Associated TeleVision (ATV) acquired a majority stake in the company in 1969. Neither the Beatles nor managers Lee Eastman and Allen Klein were able to prevent ATV from becoming majority stockholders in Northern Songs. Losing control of the company, John Lennon and Paul McCartney elected to sell their share of Northern Songs while retaining their writers' royalties. It should be noted that Sony/ATV was not a part of the 2004 joint venture between Sony and BMG.

SONY/ATV MUSIC PUBLISHING

Company: Sony/ATV Music Publishing (music publisher)
Headquarters: Santa Monica, US
Global presence: Offices in forty countries
Global market position: #5
Parent company: Sony (Japan) 50%, The Michael Jackson estate (US) 50%
Management: David Hockman (Chairman and CEO)
Administers or owns works by artists/songwriters such as:
Babyface, Brooks & Dunn, Leonard Cohen, Miles Davis, Neil Diamond, Bob Dylan, The Everly Brothers, Jimi Hendrix, Sarah McLachlan, Joni Mitchell, Graham Nash, Willie Nelson, Roy Orbison, Stephen Stills, The Beatles and Hank Williams

---

Live Nation

Live Nation is a global live music giant which is more than twice as big as AEG Live, the second-largest player of the segment. Live Nation produces, markets and sells live concerts for artists across the world. It was incorporated in 2005 through a spin-off of Clear Channel's live entertainment and sports representation businesses, and the subsequent distribution by Clear Channel of all the Live Nation common stock to its shareholders.

In 2007, Live Nation produced over 16,000 concerts for 1500 artists in fifty-seven countries, with total attendance exceeding 45 million. As of 31 December 2007, Live Nation owned, leased or operated 120 venues including 41 amphitheatres, 3 arenas and 2 festival sites. In addition, through equity, booking or similar arrangements, Live Nation has the right to book events at 27 additional venues. While most companies in the recorded music area shrank during the first decade of this century, Live Nation has had an average annual growth rate of 15 per cent since 2004. Live Nation has also developed its business into new music-related areas such as the Live Nation Artists business area launched during 2007.

This chapter has introduced the major actors in the music

LIVE NATION

Company: Live Nation (Live Music Company)
Headquarters: Beverly Hills, US
Global presence: Offices in eighteen countries
Global market position: #1
Parent company: Publicly traded at the New York Stock Exchange
Revenues (2007): $4.2 billion
Operating income: $82 million
Employees: 4700
Management: Michael Rapino (CEO)
Contracted and associated global artists: Barbra Streisand, Dave Matthews Band, Kenny Chesney, Madonna, Police, The Rolling Stones, Sting, U2, The Who etc.

industry and contextualized the ways in which the different components are connected. The next three chapters analyse different aspects of the transformation of the industry, starting with the changing relationship of music and the media in the Cloud.

3

Music and the Media

The three characteristics of the new music economy – high connectivity and little control, music provided as a service, and increased amateur creativity – are driven by the development of digital media technologies. Without digital media, there simply would be no Cloud. In this chapter I will delve deeper into some aspects of these characteristics with a particular focus on the media as the link between music and audience. This chapter deals specifically with issues related to the promotion, licensing and distribution of recorded music. I will start out by introducing a model which will support our analysis. I then continue by looking specifically at how the improved connectivity impacts on the interplay between audience, media and music. From this analysis I look at how the business of licensing recorded music has developed and I present and discuss a number of business models for selling recorded music to consumers.

The interplay between music, audience and media

Music is an integral part of most media. Movies, radio, video-games, and television all depend on music as the core or the enhancement of their products. The music industry on the other hand is completely dependent on the media, as a promoter, user and distributor of its products. Most professional musical artists communicate with their audience primarily via some kind of electronic medium and only a fraction of the audience is able to experience the artist's live performance. The dynamics of this interplay between the audience, the music and the media can be

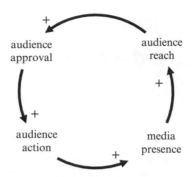

Figure 3.1 The audience–media engine (Wikström 2006)

illustrated by the 'Audience–media engine' model (Wikström 2006; 2009).[19] The model (figure 3.1) is constituted by four variables: media presence, audience reach, audience approval and audience action. Media presence represents the number of media outlets (television shows, radio shows, websites, video-games etc.) where the artist appears during a specific period of time. A music firm may try to improve its media presence through various marketing and licensing activities. Audience reach represents the percentage of the total audience which the firm is able to reach through its media presence. For instance, an appearance in a high-profile media event is able to reach a greater share of the total audience than an appearance on a media event of less significance.

Audience approval is defined as the fraction of the entire audience who respond positively when they encounter the works of a musical artist. This variable is of course affected by several other factors, but the audience–media engine focuses entirely on how audience approval is driven by the artist's presence in the media.

Audience approval is certainly important in both the old and the new music economy, but it is not able to pay the firm's bills. Rather, it is various kinds of audience actions that are tradition-ally supposed to generate the majority of the firm's revenues. The actions spurred by the audience's approval might for instance be the purchase of a song, music merchandise, concert tickets or some other music-related product. However, every action does not generate income: the making and posting of an 'Anime Music Video' on YouTube or somewhere else in the Cloud is a significant audience action but it does not generate any immediate revenues for the music firm. Rather, many music firms choose to consider such actions as an infringement of their copyrights and something which ought to be stopped entirely (these issues will discussed further in chapter 5).

Audience action also has a feedback effect on media presence. One example of this feedback from the old music economy is the logic of the 'Top 40' radio format. A radio station which follows this format plays the forty most popular songs during a certain week. 'Most popular' is in this case equal to the records which have been sold the most during the previous week. In other words, audience action, in the shape of sales at record stores, feeds back to media presence, as radio airplay.

There are many other kinds of audience action, which have the similar interplay with media presence. The structure is currently manifested all over the Cloud, for instance on social network services such as MySpace, Lala, iMeem or Bebo, but other kinds of audience actions such as fan-sites, blogs or college radio also adhere to the same logic.

The links which connect media presence, audience reach, audience approval and audience action constitute a reinforcing feedback loop which plays a crucial role in the music industry dynamics. The loop may serve as an engine which gives rise to (or ends) fads, brands, acts or genres. If the audience–media engine works against an artist or a music firm, it will be difficult or impossible to reach any kind of success. Similarly, if the music firm is able to get this loop to work in its favour, only the sky is the limit.

The ability to control the audience–media engine has been at the core of music business strategy since the very beginning of the industry. The crucial questions have been: what kind of media presence is most efficiently reaching the target audience?

Which media outlets should be used for promotion, and not be expected to generate any revenues? Vice versa, which outlets should primarily be used to collect revenues? What is the most efficient way to police copyright-infringing audience actions?

In the new music economy, characterized by high connectivity and little control, the logic of the audience–media engine is changed, and the music firms' crucial questions become increasingly difficult to answer. Below I will look into this process. I will examine the background to the loss of control and discuss its impact on the media environment by introducing the concepts of 'audience fragmentation' and 'option value blurring'. I will then link these changes to the music firm by discussing the impact on the audience–media engine.

Connectivity and control

Music is an information-based product which in its core may be considered as a *non-rival* good. In other words, a song may be consumed, or listened to, by one person without preventing simultaneous 'consumption' by others. However, by distributing music on a piece of paper, a CD or some other kind of physical carrier, it is possible to turn music into a *rival* good; to create an artificial supply deficit; control the distribution; and uphold the consumer price.

This basic principle has been supporting the music industry since the fifteenth century. Initially, sheet music was the prime vehicle for the distribution of music, and the music industry was simply just another industry among many other publishing industries such as books, magazines, newspapers etc. It was the development of new technologies such as the piano roll at the end of the nineteenth century and later cylinders, disks and a plethora of other twentieth-century storage and distribution technologies that established the new industry, separated from the traditional publishing realm (see e.g. Coleman 2003; Gronow 1983).

However, as I have discussed previously in this book, the

development of the Cloud has made it significantly more difficult to convert music into a rival good. There are numerous technologies underpinning this development, such as high-speed Internet infrastructure, data compression, peer-to-peer networking, micro-payments, mobile communications and non-volatile information storage. I will not delve into the details of any of these technologies, but will merely conclude that as a result of the development of these and other technologies the connectivity (cf. p. 5) of the network constituted by audiences and music firms is radically improved. The barriers which previously have stopped everyone, except for a few resource-rich players, from distributing information to the members of the network have almost completely disappeared.

While this development has improved the audience's access to music, it has also damaged the rights holders' ability to control the distribution of their songs on the Internet. When physical carriers become less important and Internet-based distribution gains in significance, the possibility for music firms to limit the supply of their products is rapidly diminished. Broadly speaking, rights holders of today no longer are able to control the distribution of their music. The change is irreversible. It is impossible to regain the control and limit the connectivity of the network, at least not without serious consequences for common citizens' personal integrity that few democratic governments would be willing to accept.

Audience fragmentation

As the upload capability now is more widely accessible, numerous entrepreneurs have seized the opportunity to enter the media business and launch competitors to the incumbent media outlets (see e.g. Katz 2004; Lister, Dovey et al. 2003; Thorburn & Jenkins 2003). Since the time and the resources spent by the audience on media and entertainment have not increased to the same extent, *audience fragmentation* has accelerated (see e.g. Hollifield 2003:91; Picard 2002:109–11; Simon 1971:40). In practice, this means that fewer people are tuned to the same outlet, and an appearance on a specific outlet consequently reaches a smaller part of the total audience. Audience fragmentation is closely linked to the reasoning on 'increased product variety' as presented by Brynjolfsson, Hu and Smith (2003) and popularized by Chris Anderson as 'The Long Tail' (2004; 2006). Anderson refers to the development as 'a shift from mass culture to *massively parallel culture*' (2006:184). For the music firm, this shift means that it has to place its acts in more outlets in order to uphold the level of media presence. The marketing department has to work harder, and has to spend more resources, to keep the audience–media engine going.

Option value blurring

In the old music economy, there existed a certain set of media outlets whose purpose was to expose the artist to the audience, and a distinctively different set of outlets which was used to collect revenues from that audience. All electronic media were considered to be members of the first set and physical media such as sheet music, CDs and compact cassettes as members of the second. The fundamental logic of the old music economy rests on the assumption that 'distributing' music for free via the radio and television will stimulate the demand for the same kind of music distributed via CDs and cassettes.

One way to think about these two sets of media outlets is by using the concept of option value, which was introduced in chapter 1. The music firm wants the option value of the promotion-focused outlets to be high enough for consumers to be able to appreciate the qualities of the music. On the other hand, the music firm does not want the option value of these outlets to be anywhere close to the option value of the second set. Measured on an 'option value spectrum', these two sets have to be significantly distanced from each other; otherwise the consumers will not be motivated to spend their monies buying the same music they can get for free via another medium.

The improved connectivity which has led to an increase in the number of media outlets has disrupted this old structure entirely. Cloud-based media outlets are able to vary the option value of the music they distribute ad infinitum; they are not restricted only to very high or very low levels. As a consequence there is no longer a clear distinction between 'promotion outlets' and 'distribution outlets'. A plethora of outlets have blurred the gap between the two. Many music firms have for a long time considered Internet-based music distribution as promotion with the principal purpose of stimulating sales of the real product, primarily CDs. However, in the new music economy, it has become increasingly obvious that Cloud-based music distribution not only promotes sales of music via other channels, it is also able to *satisfy* the music demand of a considerable part of the audience. Termed differently, the once strong link between exposure and sales is radically weakened.

Conclusively, improved connectivity has damaged the music firms' ability to control the flow of music and, of course, any other kind of digital information. As a consequence, numerous new media outlets have been launched which have increased the fragmentation of the audience and blurred the distinction between promotion outlets and distribution outlets.

Consequences for the audience–media engine
In spite of the changes discussed above, the structure of the audience–media engine remains the same and the links between media presence, audience reach, audience approval and audience action still hold. Without exposure in the media, there will be no audience action, which ultimately is what is feeding this business. However, even though the basic structure remains the same, the working of the audience–media engine in the new music economy is significantly different from in the old days.

For starters, the increased audience fragmentation affects the link between media presence and audience reach. The music firm has to expose its artists in more outlets in order to keep the audience reach on a constant level. This will require the firm to raise its marketing budgets which in turn will have a negative impact on profitability.

Second, the music fans' improved capability to create and upload content to the Cloud means that more audience actions will contribute to the overall exposure of the artists and add to their aggregated media presence. As a consequence, music firms have to rely more on their fans in order to create a good buzz. It also means that the clever music firm does not have to increase its marketing budget in order to compensate for the raised audience fragmentation – it can also raise its media presence by supporting its fans' desire to express themselves through the music (cf. the Trent Reznor case on p. 1).

Even though more audience actions have a positive impact on media presence, there are also fewer audience actions which actually generate immediate revenues for the music firm. As was previously discussed, a posting of a remix on YouTube, a rave review on a blog or the sharing of an artist's entire back catalogue on a peer-to-peer network might have a positive impact on the accessibility and exposure of the artist. Unfortunately, it does not have an equally positive effect on the music firm's earnings. One way to solve the problem could be to rely more on businesses which are based on the artists' ability to attract the audience's attention and enthusiasm, rather than on their willingness to take out their wallets. Such businesses could for instance be based on advertising or on licensing. One rather unusual and controversial example of such a business was manifested by a project involving the rap artist Jay-Z and the soft-drink maker Coke during 2006. Jay-Z let an eight-minute clip from a concert at Radio City Music Hall be made available on a number of peer-to-peer networks. The clip, which was downloaded more than 3.5 million times, had a short Coke ad grafted to it, which generated exposure for Coke, and monies for Jay-Z (Angwin, McBride & Smith 2006).

Since the end of the 1990s, the recorded music industry has been trying to figure out how to work the unstable and out-of-control logic of their business. The Coke–Jay-Z project is merely one example of this struggle. More than ten years into their battle the results do not look particularly impressive. However, in spite of the rather depressing outlook for music recording, other parts of the music industry are actually booming. Both the live music business and the music-licensing business have experienced several years of strong growth. In addition, the audience is still passionate about music, and many entrepreneurs, primarily outside the traditional recorded-music industry, experiment with innovative and promising business models which might be able to bring music to the fans and monies to composers and artists.

The development of the live music sector will be discussed in the next chapter which concerns the making of music on the stage and in the studio. I will in the remainder of this chapter examine the two other sectors of the industry in the light of changes discussed above.

Music licensing

Revenues from the licensing of music to various kinds of applications have always been an important part of the music business (cf. p. 58). While mechanical royalties have diminished along with the physical sales of recorded music, both performance and synchronization royalties have increased since the turn of the millennium. The graph (figure 3.2) shows the revenues of royalty-collecting societies in the UK and the US. Since the size of the markets differs, and the revenue data are measured differently, the graph has been indexed to enable comparison. Although US data are missing for the years before 2000, the graph shows that licensing revenues have doubled during the last decade.

One way to explain the boom in this part of the music industry is to point to the sudden increase in the number of media outlets discussed previously in this chapter. Media outlets without content are not very well equipped to attract audiences. Hence, content of some sort is required, and since music is an integral part of most media, the demand for music licensing has increased.

Another explanation could be a change in music firms' business

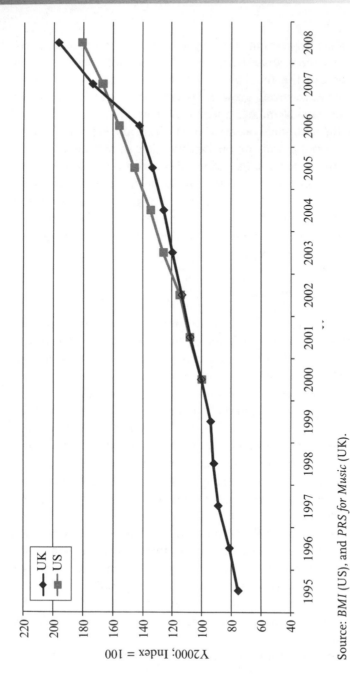

Source: *BMI* (US), and *PRS for Music* (UK).

Figure 3.2 Increase of licensing revenues 1995–2008

strategies. As audience fragmentation and other changes in the media environment make the traditional tools for music marketing and promotion less useful, music firms' marketing departments have become more interested in the use of licensing as a means to increase record sales. The licensing of a song to an advertising campaign or to a film soundtrack may achieve considerable media presence instantly. A high-profile Hollywood production aimed for the big screen usually has a marketing budget which is considerably larger than the resources allotted to album projects of the greatest of music superstars. Such resources are often able to turn even the feeblest soundtrack into a commercial success. In the advertising space, music has become an increasingly important ingredient in the production of television commercials. One example of a significant event in the history of music in advertising is the licensing of the Rolling Stone's 'Start Me Up' for almost €10 million to promote Microsoft's operating system Windows 95 worldwide (in 1995) (Graff 2003). Another example is Apple's use of Leslie Feist's '1, 2, 3, 4' in its 2007 iPod advertising. The creative use of a song in advertising can also launch an artist's career as was the case for José Gonzalez when his version of the song 'Heartbeats' was used for the Sony Bravia 'bouncing balls' commercial. Today, the days of traditional jingles is long gone, and music is now an integral component of most advertising campaigns (Korte 2005). This increased interest from advertisers and advertising agencies has established the licensing of music to commercials as a viable promotional tool. Regardless of whether the song is old or new, the media presence generated by the licensing of the song to a television commercial is hard to overestimate.

Another medium which has grown in importance as a licensee of music is the videogame. By mimicking their predecessors in the film industry, videogame producers have started to create soundtracks and license music to enhance their productions (see e.g. Schnur 2005). Black Eyed Peas, Franz Ferdinand, Good Charlotte and Pussycat Dolls are all examples of acts where a videogame has been used as an important promotional platform. A marketing manager from the videogame industry compares the marketing muscles of a global videogame brand to MTV: 'if I licensed a song in our game it will be heard up to 700 million times . . . I really provide more marketing value to a record label than MTV would do with a video . . . and our licenses are all worldwide'.

The final example of media which have created new opportunities for music licensing is mobile telephony. The significance of the mobile phone as a 'lifestyle gadget' has grown considerably since the introduction of the technology a few decades ago. As with most fashion items, a mobile device serves as a means to construct and communicate an image of the owner's identity. The actual model of the device is of course of great importance, but other signs and objects constitute the arpeggio which is messaged to the world. Music has been able to become a part of this package, in the shape of ringtones, callback tones etc.[20] There are many varieties of these sounds (e.g. voicetones, realtones, mastertones), and in all instances, a music licence is involved. The music industry has discovered that, while young music consumers are increasingly reluctant to purchase music for listening purposes, they are willing without any hesitation to spend €2 for the latest hit as a ringtone.[21]

It is important to note that this business is completely different from the traditional music business. The sounds purchased are often (but not always) based on mainstream pop music, but the consumer need which is satisfied by these products is completely different from the need which is satisfied by 'ordinary' music.

It is difficult to find reliable estimates of the size of the global ringtone market. Those numbers that circulate estimated the size of the European market to $1.1 billion and the US market to $550 million during 2007. Although the size of the ringtone business may be impressive, from a technical perspective its longevity is questionable. Since 2007 the size of the market has flattened and in some markets started to shrink. This development has been expected for some time since mobile devices are increasingly able to use ordinarily formatted songs as ringtones and the need to purchase specifically formatted songs is decreasing.

Music licensing has always been an integral and lucrative part of the music business, but it has often created a tension in the relationships between music publishers and record labels. Although music is the essential factor to both of them, their aims and their business models differ. To the music publisher or the licensing department of a full-service music firm, licensing opportunities such as the ones discussed above are the bread and butter of their business. There is simply no other kind of income besides the royalties paid by the licensees. From the record labels' point of view, the licensing has a completely different purpose, and that purpose is to promote an act. The licensing fee paid by the licensee is only the icing on the cake, since the record label's core business is the selling of audio recordings (primarily CDs) to consumers. In a competition to have a song included in a film etc., the record label might be inclined to waive the fee in order to win the competition and achieve the much desired media presence.

Media outlets often play the 'promotion card' when negotiating terms of music content licensing. The media outlet argues that the music firm should waive the licence fee since the outlet is promoting the artist and the song. A music publisher explains: 'this is a perennial argument that I had with MTV. . . you can argue that most uses of music are promotion, but you have to draw the line . . . you can't give it away free, and the record companies, unfortunately, are being too willing to give music away for free'.

When licensing music to a commercial, an advertiser or an advertising agency is the licensee, and often uses the same argument as a media outlet. Another music publisher reflects on the situation:

> what is happening in the advertising world is concerning . . . sometimes advertisers want to use very cutting edge music . . . and it is seen as an opportunity by everyone to break a band, break a new song . . . [advertisers] are beginning to turn around and say 'you know I are breaking your band and I shouldn't have to pay to use the music' . . . there never used to be any question that the advertiser was expected to pay for the

music . . . but I think it has happened during the last two or
three years.

The intense skirmishing in the licensing negotiations has so far
not shown any signs of subsiding. It is interesting to note that even
in those cases where the music publisher and the record label are
parts of the same organization, conflicts are just as prevalent.

The diminishing of the revenues from sales of recorded music
impacts on the negotiations between the rights holders and the
potential licensees. The licensees' traditional claim that the fee
should be reduced since the rights holders will earn their money
on sales of recorded music is no longer very solid. A quote from
a record label executive indicates how rights holders demand
higher royalties from media outlets to compensate for the
reduced sales of recorded music products.

> TV and radio has built their business models on the assump-
> tion that they have access to free content from content owners.
> Content owners have assumed that to be promotion for their
> physical products. However, since physical product sales are
> going down, content owners have begun to demand royalties for
> the use of their content on outlets such as radio, TV, etc.

This clash between rights holders and licensees will intensify as
the transformation of the media environment continues. The
rights holders in the music industry will most likely take the lead
in this process since their situation is a notch more desperate than
that of the media outlets. Based on the reasoning brought forward
by this study, the rights holders' argument weighs somewhat
heavier than the argument from the licensees. Consequently,
when negotiating the fee for using a song in a particular set-
ting, the potential promotional value of the exposure should not
be exaggerated. The fee should primarily be determined by the
artistic value the song brings to the licensee and should only be
minutely influenced by the promotional value the exposure may
bring back to the owner of the intellectual property.

Music publishers challenge the record labels' domain

The growing revenue from music licensing changes the position and purpose of the music publisher within the new music economy. The music publishers, which for decades have been reduced to the record labels' side-kick, have regained some of their original status. This process has been predicted by several scholars, for instance by Wallis (1995), but the change is no longer in the future but is rather a matter of fact. Several observations show how the role of the publisher is changing. Besides the growing revenues from performance and synchronization royalties it is also interesting to note how tasks that previously were a part of the record labels' domain increasingly are performed by music publishers. One such example is the control of the master recording.[22] Traditionally, music publishers have controlled the composition and the lyrics on behalf of the songwriter while the record label has controlled the actual recording on behalf of the performer. During recent years it has become increasingly common that artists employ a music publisher to control not only the composition but also the recording. This enables the music publisher to act in new ways. The music publisher is able to license the recording for various purposes, without the need to involve a record label. Since music licensing is the core business of the music publisher, the publisher is often more capable and motivated than a licensing department at the record label in getting the most licensing monies out of a certain intellectual property. A medium-sized US-based music publisher explains:

> there is a need to exploit the master side as well . . . it is not very different from the publishing side when you come to think about things [*sic*] as synchronization and even some new media . . . so I then have to put on our record label hat for a little while . . . so essentially it's a necessity . . . for our clients they need someone to look after both sides and why not have us do it . . . it makes sense . . . being in control of publishing and the master side is very helpful, particularly in the new media where companies want to deal with one entity.

The control of the master recording also enables the music publisher to act as a record label in areas other than the licensing domain. The decreased risk willingness among some music firms, especially record labels, has made the labels' A&R process slow and bureaucratic. Some music publishers have reacted to the record labels' revised A&R strategies by cutting the labels completely out of the loop to release the records themselves. When physical distribution is required in a project, the music publisher may contract a record label to handle distribution, but if the song is to be exclusively distributed via the Internet, no involvement whatsoever from a label is required.

Other similar trends are discernible among music publishers. For instance, when record labels are reluctant to invest in new performer talent, opportunities have been opened up to music publishers. Some publishers have decided to nourish inexperienced performers' careers in a way which is similar to traditional record label activities:

> I think you really have to go back to the days of the Brill Building years and the Tin Pan Alley, when there was no record labels because there were no records yet . . . the publishers were actually the promotional force behind the artist, because there was no medium outside the piano roll and the sheet music and it was the publishers that sort of peddled, they went door to door and promoted . . . the record labels came in and then that kind of significantly changed . . . they took over that role of peddling and promoting acts . . . and now I view it as trying to go back, to a certain degree.

Conclusively, not only is the revenue stream from the licensing business growing in importance, in addition, the role of the music publishers is changing and is challenging the traditional domain of the record labels. While the record labels are on the retreat, music publishers are on the advance, and it is no longer obvious where the line between a record label and a music publisher should be drawn.

Recorded music

In the previous section I discussed how music licensing is gaining in importance at the expense of recorded music. Today it is almost a matter of fact that sales of recorded music are a dying business and the new music economy is primarily based on revenues from licensing and concerts (see e.g. Goodman 2008). However, consumers' demand for recorded music is greater than ever. While the worldwide sales of music CDs have dropped rapidly since 2000, the total number of songs acquired by consumers legally or illegally via various peer-to-peer networks has dramatically increased. It is estimated that, for every track legally downloaded online, twenty songs are being illegally downloaded from peer-to-peer networks (IFPJ 2008). The question is whether it is possible to transform the 'online pirates' into legitimate users of legal online music services. Today, there are numerous legitimate services in the Cloud, all experimenting with different business models and revenues models, all looking for the 'killer app' that is able to attract the young and restless. I will in this section look at a number of those services and revenue models and analyse the potential sustainability of their businesses.

Single-song download

Online music sales during 2007 were estimated to $2.9 billion and accounted for 15 per cent of the global recorded music market. There are more than 500 digital music services worldwide sharing these revenues, but the market is heavily dominated by one player, Apple iTunes Store. iTunes is an online service which carries millions of songs, thousands of audiobooks and music videos and hundreds of television shows and movies in its catalogue. The service is developed and operated by the computer manufacturer Apple which in 2003, under the leadership of Steve Jobs, was able to convince all the majors to provide their music to the iTunes service. iTunes was the first service at the time to offer single songs for download, unbundled from the album and without requiring the consumer to sign up for a monthly subscription.

During the first years of running the service, iTunes followed a very clear strategy based on two principles: uniform pricing and system lock-in. *Uniform pricing* means that every song in the catalogue is sold at the same price, for instance in the US, 99 cents. This pricing structure is of course extremely easy to understand and to communicate, which facilitated the successful introduction of the service. The second principle of the Apple iTunes initial strategy is related to the fact that iTunes really is part of a larger business model which also includes other Apple products, primarily the portable media player, iPod. Initially, iTunes used a proprietary copy-protection technology (DRM) called Fairplay which restricted consumers from playing the music they had acquired on iTunes on any portable device other than the Apple iPod. If consumers decided to switch to another non-Apple portable music player, they had to purchase the same songs all over again. This business strategy is referred to as *system lock-in* and is aimed to make it difficult and expensive for those customers who want to change to another, competing technology (see e.g. Hax & Wilde 2001; Shapiro & Varian 1999).

Apple's initial strategy and well-crafted marketing campaigns reached an incredible level of success. In January 2008, music sales on iTunes constituted more than 70 per cent of the global legal online music market, with billions of songs and millions of iPods sold worldwide. Apple iTunes Store is currently the largest music retailer in the US, even including the brick-and-mortar retailing giant Wal-Mart.

Starting in 2007, the iTunes strategy was increasingly challenged. Record labels tried to convince Apple to reconsider its pricing policy and to use a tiered pricing model rather than the uniform model. In addition, Apple's aggressive lock-in strategy was criticized by consumer organizations, governments and record labels. The conflicts between labels and Apple actually caused the largest multinational music firm, Universal Music Group, to refuse to extend its existing long-term agreement with

Apple. However, since iTunes have such a dominating market position it was impossible even for Universal to remove their songs from the iTunes catalogue completely. Hence, Universal chose to sign a short-term agreement which currently is updated on a frequent basis.

As an answer to these complaints, another influential player, one of the world's largest online retailers, Amazon, entered the single-song download market in September 2007. Amazon offers single tracks using a tiered pricing structure and without any proprietary DRM. Eventually the pressure from Amazon, record labels and other parties forced Apple to abandon its initial strategy and since spring 2009 it offers its entire catalogue without DRM, and different prices.

Memberships – limited download quota
The second-largest online music retailer is called eMusic, and it uses a slightly different model from Apple iTunes. eMusic has, since a number of years back, offered its music without proprietary DRM, a decision which eventually has proved to be quite clever. Since many major record labels have worried that they might lose control of their songs if they don't use copy-protection technologies, eMusic has not been able to get any one of the four majors to sign up to their service. As a consequence, eMusic decided to focus on a slightly older target audience by adding artists signed by smaller labels within genres such as jazz, blues and classic rock.

eMusic's relationship with its customers is also somewhat different from Apple iTunes'. eMusic offer a membership and three different plans which allow the consumers to download a specified number of tracks per month. This model is not a digital innovation, but has been used many times by various media companies, in the shape of 'Book-of-the-month clubs', 'record clubs', etc. These kinds of models make the revenue flow to the service provider more stable and predictable compared with the single-song download model. As a result, the service provider is able to offer the products for a significantly lower price. While a track at iTunes US is priced at 99 cents, the price of a track at eMusic in the same territory might be as low as 28 cents.

The royalties paid by eMusic to rights holders is based on quite a different model from that of the single-song-download retailers. While Apple iTunes and Amazon pay their supplier based on a fixed wholesale price, eMusic pays rights holders based on a revenue-sharing model. Half of the revenues from subscriptions are added to a pool of money. These monies are then paid out to rights holders based on the number of downloads of their songs.

Memberships – all-you-can-eat
Another kind of membership model which is quite different from the one manifested by eMusic is the all-you-can-eat model. This model gives members unlimited on-demand access to a large music catalogue. Members are able to download songs and depending on which membership plan they have signed up to, they may also be able to play the songs on portable media players. Different versions of this model have been implemented by services such as MelOn, Omnifone and MusicStation, Rhapsody and Spotify. It is important to emphasize that these kinds of services only give consumers temporary licences to listen to the music.

These services have been available for some years, but, so far, they have not been particularly successful. This might seem a bit mysterious since the services, compared with many other models, offer substantially better value for money by offering unlimited access to music for less than $15 per month. One reason might be that, although this is very good value for money, the concept of the temporary licences still is difficult for consumers to accept. The illusion of being able to 'own your music', which has been the concept since the advent of the first recording technologies, is difficult to replace with a concept of 'music as a service' or 'music rentals'. I will return to this issue later in this chapter.

One tricky question with the all-you-can-eat models is how to split the revenues between the owners of the copyrights. One option is to base the split on the number of downloads during a specific month – which would be identical to the eMusic revenue-sharing model. Although that principle would be clear and simple, it would not be suitable for the all-you-can-eat model. It is more appropriate to split the revenues based on which songs currently are licensed by the consumers during a specific period. A third model makes the split based on *usage* rather than on downloads. Assume that a consumer is curious about jazz music and downloads every jazz song she can find in the catalogue. Eventually she learns that it is only ten of the downloaded songs she actually likes and listens to. The other ones she does not fancy and they simply remain on her hard drive without being touched. It then seems fairer to split the revenues only between the rights holder of the ten songs she likes and not between the owners of the hundreds of songs she happened to download during her discovery process. However, there is a downside to the third revenue-sharing principle since it requires the collection of detailed usage statistics on an individual level. Since that might threaten the consumer's personal integrity it is important that any identifier is removed from the usage data uploaded from the member to the service provider.[23]

Ad-based models

All the models discussed so far are based on revenue streams directly from the music listening audience. But these services are not very successful in competing with the free (but illegal) services available 'two clicks away'. One way to compete with free services might be to create a business model which collects revenues from sources other than the audience. If such a service is crafted in a clever way the music will feel like free to the music audience, and, hence, the incentive to use the illegal services is removed.

'Feels-like-free' music services are far from a new phenomenon. In the old music economy these services were called commercial broadcast radio stations and played a very important role as taste-makers and promotion tools for the record labels of the time.

The digital versions of these services are available in a range of flavours all offering different option values. The vanilla flavour is basically a carbon copy of the traditional commercial broadcast radio model, merely transferred to the Internet platform. Music and any other content is not downloaded to the listener, but is *streamed*[24] from the service provider. As in the case of traditional broadcast radio, the programming follows a playlist which the listener is unable to manipulate immediately. Record labels have no problems getting their heads around these kinds of services. The services fit well in the old music industry logic where music was exposed in one media outlet in order to raise the demand for the same kind of music distributed via a physical carrier.

Ad-based music services which offer an option value slightly higher than the service presented above enable the listener to *personalize* the playlist in some way or another (Pandora, last.fm, etc.). One mechanism could simply be to allow the user to ask for a song to be added to the playlist by sending a request to the service provider. Another, somewhat more sophisticated mechanism is to create playlists based on the preferences and behaviour of a large number of users. Based on such aggregated usage data, it is possible to predict what other kinds of music fans of a specific artist are likely to appreciate. In addition, these personalization mechanisms are often combined with other tools which allow the service to learn what kind of music the user likes or not. Based on this and other kinds of usage data, it is possible to create playlists which are extremely well tuned to the tastes of specific listeners. Thereby it is possible to create a personalized and appealing music experience even though the service lacks on-demand capability and the listener is unable to decide exactly which song should be played at a particular point in time.

Besides being able to play songs which the listeners are very likely to appreciate, the collection of the detailed usage data enables the service provider to charge a premium for targeted advertising, and thereby to increase the likelihood of the service ever reaching break-even. From the rights holders' perspective, even this service fits relatively well into their traditional way of categorizing various media technologies as either a promotion tool or as a music distribution technology. In this case the ad-based personalized streaming services are categorized as promotion tools and taste-makers, rather than a potential substitution to actual downloads or CD sales. However, the question is whether they really are making the correct judgement. The services are doing an excellent job as taste-makers and are in one sense stimulating the listener's music awareness. However, the structure and features of the services enable them to *satisfy* the listeners' music demand and to reduce the demand for the same music distributed via high-option-value technologies. Apparently these services provide illustrative examples of music services which it is not possible to categorize as either promoting sales or substituting sales. These services belong to both sets at the same time.

Going one step further along the option-value spectrum, I find ad-based services which actually offer music on demand (e.g. Spotify). Regardless whether the distribution principle is 'download' or 'streaming', the users are able to listen to the music of their choice whenever they want. From the rights holders' point of view, this kind of on-demand music service is identical to the single-song-download model. Since listeners are able to listen to whatever music they want, whenever they want, this is no longer a promotion tool; it is a music distribution technology. Based on that understanding, many rights holders argue that they need a much higher compensation from the service providers compared to what they request from providers of playlist-based services.

Apple's iTunes agreements, which offer rights holders about 60 cents per download, have evolved into the industry benchmark for record label/online retailer agreements. The problem is that there are no ad-based business models which are able to generate enough revenues to cover such high licensing fees.

The providers of ad-based music services try to convince the rights holders that these services should not be compared to the deals made with iTunes and the like. Rather, as the service providers claim to be able to pull the audience away from illegal file-sharing activities, they argue that the revenues from these services should be compared to zero cents per download rather than with 60 cents per download. Hence, labels ought to be happy with a revenue-sharing model, based on revenues from advertising sales.

Even though rights holders are extremely reluctant to accept that reasoning, some agreements between rights holders and providers of ad-based music on-demand services have been made. So far the majority of these agreements have not been in the service provider's favour. First, the service provider has to pay a fee for each stream which is served *in addition* to a considerable chunk of the advertising revenues. Second, some of the major music firms have also demanded an equity position in the service provider's limited company. Third, to ensure that the music firm does not have to carry any risk whatsoever, the service provider is required to make a large prepayment from which future payments are supposed to be deducted.

If businesses are based on such agreements between rights holders and services providers, it is unlikely that they ever will reach profitability. A financial analysis of the business case shows that the revenues generated simply will not be enough to support a stable and profitable company. Indeed, it is understandable that the rights holders are reluctant to let the revenues from the service be based on the hope that the service provider is capable of building a profitable advertising business. Many experienced entrepreneurs have miserably failed with such endeavours. Looking at the development within the illegal sphere of the online music scene, and at the infinitesimal likelihood of the rights holders ever being able to regain control of that sphere, it does strike me as somewhat strange that the rights holders decline the prospect of some additional revenues. However, there are some signs that rights holders might be willing to reconsider

Bundling music with other media products

The practice of grouping products or services into a set which then is marketed and sold as a single package is a marketing strategy referred to as 'product bundling'. The practice is common in many industries, for instance in the cable television industry where consumers often are required to subscribe to a whole set of channels even if they are only interested in one of them. It is also a common practice in the music industry where the full-length album is the well-established way to bundle a set of songs.

Another bundling model which is getting increasingly common is to bundle various products with specific issues of magazines or newspapers. Such 'covermounts' have developed into a very important promotion opportunity for the music industry and likewise an important way for the magazine publishers to enhance the value of their product. The bundling strategy is, however, not only restricted to these combinations. Recorded music is for obvious reasons linked to devices for music listening, both portable and stationary. Since 1997, when the first portable digital audio players with large non-volatile internal memory reached the market, it has become common practice to pre-load these players with some kind of music. In most cases, this kind of bundling is not very sophisticated. A handful of tracks are simply pre-loaded onto the device to ensure that there is something to listen to immediately when the consumer pulls the device out of the packaging. However, there are some cases which are more interesting. One such case was the cooperation between the Irish rock band U2 and Apple. The cooperation ᵗᵉd for several years and included among other things the ᵐmitment from U2 to actively participate in the marketing ᵒᶠ iPod and iTunes products. However, the most visible part ᵒᶠ ᵖroject was a specially designed iPod, engraved with the ᵐembers' autographs and bundled with all the music (400 ᵒʳ recorded by U2.[25]

ʰigh-end mobile phones now have digital audio play-ᵉʳ, the practice of pre-loading or bundling music with ᵇeen adopted by mobile handset manufacturers.

their stance and sign contracts which are viable to both parties. This will be further discussed in the final chapter.

Value-based pricing models

There are other, somewhat more exotic revenue models which may or may not be workable, but still are interesting objects of analysis. Most of these models centre on the concept of value-based pricing, that is to charge for a service or product in relation to the value delivered to the customer. Value-based pricing is interesting when applied to the music business since the value music gives to people may be very different. The song which moves one person to tears may be perceived as totally uninspiring to another. In such a scenario, how should a value-based pricing scheme be implemented?

One way to attack the issue is to ask listeners to pay whatever they think is the appropriate amount, known as the Tip Jar model. If that amount is zero, then the listener does not have to pay anything at all. One small record label has tried to create a business based on this principle. The record label is Magnatune, founded by John Buckman in 2003. Magnatune splits its revenues 50/50 with the rights holders whose music they offer. Magnatune offers the music in various kinds of packages, also as single-song downloads. The difference between this and other single-song-download services is that the consumers are able to choose how much they should pay for the music they download, ranging between 5 and 18 US dollars. The Magnatune service has been up and running for some time, but it is not doing very well. One reason may be the lack of promotion, another that the music catalogue primarily consists of unsigned and relatively unknown artists. As with many of the somewhat more unusual models, the major record labels have not shown any interest in being part of the experiment.

It is highly unlikely that Tip Jar models will become anything more than a curiosity among recorded music pricing models. Even though the average price people pay will be above zero, the additional unpredictability which the model adds to the business is not exactly what music firms currently are looking for.

CASE STUDY: RADIOHEAD – *IN RAINBOWS*

Radiohead is one of the world's most successful rock bands with a career spanning more than two decades. On 10 October 2007, Radiohead had ended its contract with EMI Group and was able to decide how, where and when their newly recorded *In Rainbows* should be released. Rather than releasing the album through the traditional distribution channels, Radiohead offered the album as a download on its website. In a very unconventional move, the band allowed fans to pay what they wanted for the album: even nothing. The Radiohead front man, Thom Yorke, explains: 'Every record for the last four – including my solo record – has been leaked. So the idea was like, we'll leak it, then' (Byrne & Yorke 2007). Interestingly, many fans did pay for the album. According to the Internet market research company comScore, the album was downloaded approximately 1 million times and 40 per cent of the downloading fans paid on average $6 for the download. This means that the average revenue per download was $2.40, which most likely is more than the share they would have received during their EMI contract.

The experiment lasted for two months and the album was released via traditional channels in January 2008. One year after being 'leaked' on the band's own website, *In Rainbows* had sold 3 million copies; it had reached the No. 1 spot in the US *Billboard* 200 and in the UK album chart. In 2009, the album won two Grammy Awards for Best Alternative Music Album and Best Special Limited Edition Package. Even though the experiment was probably profitable for the band, it should perhaps be considered as a promotional gimmick rather than a sustainable pricing and distribution strategy. The band's manager, Bryce Edge, explained right after the release of the album that: 'In November I have to start with the mass market plans and get them under way. If I didn't believe that when people hear the music they will want to buy the CD, then I wouldn't do what I are doing. This is a solution for Radiohead, not for the industry' (Barrett 2007).

A more viable alternative to the Tip Jar model is to offer music to consumers in differently priced packages aimed to appeal to different consumer categories. This kind of pricing strategy is normally termed 'versioning' or 'quality discrimination' and is a common practice for products such as travel, software or many other Cloud-based services. Airline travel

---

VERSIONING *GHOSTS I–IV*

The Trent Reznor case presented on p. 1 is also an example of quality discrimination, as Reznor offered the recording in five different versions:

Free	The first nine tracks from the *Ghosts I–IV* collection available as high-quality, DRM-free MP3s, including the complete PDF.
$5	All thirty-six tracks in a variety of digital formats including a forty-page PDF.
$10	2 × CD set: *Ghosts I–IV* on two audio CDs in a six-panel digipak package with a sixteen-page booklet. Includes immediate full download in a variety of digital formats.
$75	Deluxe Edition Package: *Ghosts I–IV* in a hardcover fabric slipcase containing: 2 audio CDs, 1 data DVD with all thirty-six tracks in multitrack format, and a Blu-ray disc with *Ghosts I–IV* in high-definition 96/24 stereo and accompanying slideshow. Includes immediate download in a variety of digital formats.
$300	Ultra Deluxe Limited Edition Package: includes everything you get for $75, plus an exclusive four-LP 180 gram vinyl set in a fabric slipcase, and two exclusive limited edition Giclée prints in a luxurious package. The package is limited to only 2500, and each one is signed by Reznor himself.

is offered as Economy, Business or First; software as Home, Small Business or Ultimate; and Cloud-base[d] tion services as Basic, Plus or Premium. In the c[ase] more particularly a specific set of songs, th[e] to differentiate the quality of the produ[ct] the packaging or the quality of sou[nd] by providing access to 'extra m[aterial] importance, the value of t[he] manipulating the opti[ons] of how versioning [...] recorded music indu[stry] Timberlake album *Fut[ureSex]* of 2006. One hundred [...] have been created from the [...] than 19 million units worldw[ide] CDs (IFPI 2008).

The world's largest handset manufacturer, Nokia, launched an extensive bundling program titled 'Comes With Music' in 2008. The program gives people who purchase certain Nokia phones 'unlimited' access to a music catalogue during twelve months. The option value of this offering is fairly limited, since the downloaded songs are not transferable to other handsets. Nevertheless, it is notable that the songs are offered with a permanent licence and will remain useful and listenable after the end of the twelve-month period. To be able to offer permanent licences and unlimited access to music from all four majors, Nokia most probably have to pay hefty amounts to the rights holders for every handset sold, and it is unlikely that this program ever will be profitable on a stand-alone basis. Rather it should be considered as an aggressive way for Nokia to get a foothold in the music business. In parallel with the 'Comes With Music' program, Nokia has launched a music service by the name Ovi, where music, movies and other information products will be offered according to the single-song-download model. The purpose of the 'Comes With Music' program probably is to get the Ovi service off the ground. It remains to be seen if the strategy will be successful.

Nokia is not the only handset manufacturer which has shown interest in the music business. For instance, the Nokia competitors Sony Ericsson and LG have also announced similar programs and services. These initiatives are all part of a major industrial transformation where the telecommunication industry is moving closer to the music and entertainment industries. In the next section I will take a look at this process of industrial convergence.

Mobile music
Since 1981, when the world's first fully automatic mobile telephony service was launched in Scandinavia, wireless communications have come a long way. Today there are more than 3.3 billion mobile telephone subscribers worldwide and this new infrastructure rapidly transforms the way people travel, socialize, do business and – listen to music.

The two most important drivers of profits in the mobile telephony business are the average revenue per user (ARPU) and churn, i.e. the proportion of the subscribers who leave the service during a given time period. All mobile telephony operators strive to keep their ARPU as high as possible and their churn as low as possible. One way of achieving these goals is to offer the users long-term subscription plans and add-on services which encourage customer loyalty and stimulate users to spend their entertainment monies through their mobile phones.

While the mobile telephony operators hunger for services which increase ARPU and customer loyalty, the recorded music industry is for obvious reasons in a fairly desperate position. By combining the strengths of the two industries, the hope is that both their respective wishes will be fulfilled. In the most advanced mobile telephony markets around the world – particularly in Northeast Asia and in Europe – mobile operators and music companies have embraced each other. One such example is SK Telecom, the largest mobile telephony operator in South Korea with more than 20 million subscribers. SK Telecom has moved into the music industry by acquiring a leading South Korean record label, JYP Entertainment, and a major Korean distributor, Seoul Records. They also operate MelOn, the country's largest online music service with more than 4 million basic subscribers and 600,000 premium subscribers paying a monthly fee of $5 for an all-you-can-eat music offering.

Among the models which have been presented in this chapter, the all-you-can-eat model is by far the most appealing model to package with a traditional mobile telephony subscription plan. For instance, it is a very straightforward task to add such a service into the mobile telephony operator's billing system, while a music service based on the single-song-download model is far more complex to integrate with a mobile operator's subscription-based business structure.

It is very likely that, within only a few years from now, most mobile telephony operators, at least in the world's more advanced mobile markets, will have an all-you-can-eat music service as a their stance and sign contracts which are viable to both parties. This will be further discussed in the final chapter.

Value-based pricing models

There are other, somewhat more exotic revenue models which may or may not be workable, but still are interesting objects of analysis. Most of these models centre on the concept of value-based pricing, that is to charge for a service or product in relation to the value delivered to the customer. Value-based pricing is interesting when applied to the music business since the value music gives to people may be very different. The song which moves one person to tears may be perceived as totally uninspiring to another. In such a scenario, how should a value-based pricing scheme be implemented?

One way to attack the issue is to ask listeners to pay whatever they think is the appropriate amount, known as the Tip Jar model. If that amount is zero, then the listener does not have to pay anything at all. One small record label has tried to create a business based on this principle. The record label is Magnatune, founded by John Buckman in 2003. Magnatune splits its revenues 50/50 with the rights holders whose music they offer. Magnatune offers the music in various kinds of packages, also as single-song downloads. The difference between this and other single-song-download services is that the consumers are able to choose how much they should pay for the music they download, ranging between 5 and 18 US dollars. The Magnatune service has been up and running for some time, but it is not doing very well. One reason may be the lack of promotion, another that the music catalogue primarily consists of unsigned and relatively unknown artists. As with many of the somewhat more unusual models, the major record labels have not shown any interest in being part of the experiment.

It is highly unlikely that Tip Jar models will become anything more than a curiosity among recorded music pricing models. Even though the average price people pay will be above zero, the additional unpredictability which the model adds to the business is not exactly what music firms currently are looking for.

CASE STUDY: RADIOHEAD – *IN RAINBOWS*

Radiohead is one of the world's most successful rock bands with a career spanning more than two decades. On 10 October 2007, Radiohead had ended its contract with EMI Group and was able to decide how, where and when their newly recorded *In Rainbows* should be released. Rather than releasing the album through the traditional distribution channels, Radiohead offered the album as a download on its website. In a very unconventional move, the band allowed fans to pay what they wanted for the album: even nothing. The Radiohead front man, Thom Yorke, explains: 'Every record for the last four – including my solo record – has been leaked. So the idea was like, we'll leak it, then' (Byrne & Yorke 2007). Interestingly, many fans did pay for the album. According to the Internet market research company comScore, the album was downloaded approximately 1 million times and 40 per cent of the downloading fans paid on average $6 for the download. This means that the average revenue per download was $2.40, which most likely is more than the share they would have received during their EMI contract.

The experiment lasted for two months and the album was released via traditional channels in January 2008. One year after being 'leaked' on the band's own website, *In Rainbows* had sold 3 million copies; it had reached the No. 1 spot in the US *Billboard* 200 and in the UK album chart. In 2009, the album won two Grammy Awards for Best Alternative Music Album and Best Special Limited Edition Package. Even though the experiment was probably profitable for the band, it should perhaps be considered as a promotional gimmick rather than a sustainable pricing and distribution strategy. The band's manager, Bryce Edge, explained right after the release of the album that: 'In November I have to start with the mass market plans and get them under way. If I didn't believe that when people hear the music they will want to buy the CD, then I wouldn't do what I are doing. This is a solution for Radiohead, not for the industry' (Barrett 2007).

A more viable alternative to the Tip Jar model is to offer music to consumers in differently priced packages aimed to appeal to different consumer categories. This kind of pricing strategy is normally termed 'versioning' or 'quality discrimination' and is a common practice for products such as travel, software or many other Cloud-based services. Airline travel

---

VERSIONING *GHOSTS I–IV*

The Trent Reznor case presented on p. 1 is also an example of quality discrimination, as Reznor offered the recording in five different versions:

Free   The first nine tracks from the *Ghosts I–IV* collection available as high-quality, DRM-free MP3s, including the complete PDF.

$5   All thirty-six tracks in a variety of digital formats including a forty-page PDF.

$10   2 × CD set: *Ghosts I–IV* on two audio CDs in a six-panel digipak package with a sixteen-page booklet. Includes immediate full download in a variety of digital formats.

$75   Deluxe Edition Package: *Ghosts I–IV* in a hardcover fabric slipcase containing: 2 audio CDs, 1 data DVD with all thirty-six tracks in multitrack format, and a Blu-ray disc with *Ghosts I–IV* in high-definition 96/24 stereo and accompanying slideshow. Includes immediate download in a variety of digital formats.

$300   Ultra Deluxe Limited Edition Package: includes everything you get for $75, plus an exclusive four-LP 180 gram vinyl set in a fabric slipcase, and two exclusive limited edition Giclée prints in a luxurious package. The package is limited to only 2500, and each one is signed by Reznor himself.

---

is offered as Economy, Business or First; software as Basic, Home, Small Business or Ultimate; and Cloud-based information services as Basic, Plus or Premium. In the case of music, or more particularly a specific set of songs, there are several ways to differentiate the quality of the product, such as by changing the packaging or the quality of sound, by limiting the supply or by providing access to 'extra material'. In addition, and of equal importance, the value of the music can of course be varied by manipulating the option value. There are numerous examples of how versioning strategies are increasingly applied to the recorded music industry. One high-profile example is the Justin Timberlake album *FutureSex/LoveSounds* released in September of 2006. One hundred and fifteen different products/versions have been created from the project which in total has sold more than 19 million units worldwide. Only 20 per cent of these were CDs (IFPI 2008).

Bundling music with other media products

The practice of grouping products or services into a set which then is marketed and sold as a single package is a marketing strategy referred to as 'product bundling'. The practice is common in many industries, for instance in the cable television industry where consumers often are required to subscribe to a whole set of channels even if they are only interested in one of them. It is also a common practice in the music industry where the full-length album is the well-established way to bundle a set of songs.

Another bundling model which is getting increasingly common is to bundle various products with specific issues of magazines or newspapers. Such 'covermounts' have developed into a very important promotion opportunity for the music industry and likewise an important way for the magazine publishers to enhance the value of their product. The bundling strategy is, however, not only restricted to these combinations. Recorded music is for obvious reasons linked to devices for music listening, both portable and stationary. Since 1997, when the first portable digital audio players with large non-volatile internal memory reached the market, it has become common practice to pre-load these players with some kind of music. In most cases, this kind of bundling is not very sophisticated. A handful of tracks are simply pre-loaded onto the device to ensure that there is something to listen to immediately when the consumer pulls the device out of the packaging. However, there are some cases which are more interesting. One such case was the cooperation between the Irish rock band U2 and Apple. The cooperation lasted for several years and included among other things the commitment from U2 to actively participate in the marketing of the iPod and iTunes products. However, the most visible part of the project was a specially designed iPod, engraved with the band members' autographs and bundled with all the music (400 tracks) ever recorded by U2.[25]

As most high-end mobile phones now have digital audio playback capability, the practice of pre-loading or bundling music with hardware has been adopted by mobile handset manufacturers.

The world's largest handset manufacturer, Nokia, launched an extensive bundling program titled 'Comes With Music' in 2008. The program gives people who purchase certain Nokia phones 'unlimited' access to a music catalogue during twelve months. The option value of this offering is fairly limited, since the downloaded songs are not transferable to other handsets. Nevertheless, it is notable that the songs are offered with a permanent licence and will remain useful and listenable after the end of the twelve-month period. To be able to offer permanent licences and unlimited access to music from all four majors, Nokia most probably have to pay hefty amounts to the rights holders for every handset sold, and it is unlikely that this program ever will be profitable on a stand-alone basis. Rather it should be considered as an aggressive way for Nokia to get a foothold in the music business. In parallel with the 'Comes With Music' program, Nokia has launched a music service by the name Ovi, where music, movies and other information products will be offered according to the single-song-download model. The purpose of the 'Comes With Music' program probably is to get the Ovi service off the ground. It remains to be seen if the strategy will be successful.

Nokia is not the only handset manufacturer which has shown interest in the music business. For instance, the Nokia competitors Sony Ericsson and LG have also announced similar programs and services. These initiatives are all part of a major industrial transformation where the telecommunication industry is moving closer to the music and entertainment industries. In the next section I will take a look at this process of industrial convergence.

Mobile music

Since 1981, when the world's first fully automatic mobile telephony service was launched in Scandinavia, wireless communications have come a long way. Today there are more than 3.3 billion mobile telephone subscribers worldwide and this new infrastructure rapidly transforms the way people travel, socialize, do business and – listen to music.

The two most important drivers of profits in the mobile telephony business are the average revenue per user (ARPU) and churn, i.e. the proportion of the subscribers who leave the service during a given time period. All mobile telephony operators strive to keep their ARPU as high as possible and their churn as low as possible. One way of achieving these goals is to offer the users long-term subscription plans and add-on services which encourage customer loyalty and stimulate users to spend their entertainment monies through their mobile phones.

While the mobile telephony operators hunger for services which increase ARPU and customer loyalty, the recorded music industry is for obvious reasons in a fairly desperate position. By combining the strengths of the two industries, the hope is that both their respective wishes will be fulfilled. In the most advanced mobile telephony markets around the world – particularly in Northeast Asia and in Europe – mobile operators and music companies have embraced each other. One such example is SK Telecom, the largest mobile telephony operator in South Korea with more than 20 million subscribers. SK Telecom has moved into the music industry by acquiring a leading South Korean record label, JYP Entertainment, and a major Korean distributor, Seoul Records. They also operate MelOn, the country's largest online music service with more than 4 million basic subscribers and 600,000 premium subscribers paying a monthly fee of $5 for an all-you-can-eat music offering.

Among the models which have been presented in this chapter, the all-you-can-eat model is by far the most appealing model to package with a traditional mobile telephony subscription plan. For instance, it is a very straightforward task to add such a service into the mobile telephony operator's billing system, while a music service based on the single-song-download model is far more complex to integrate with a mobile operator's subscription-based business structure.

It is very likely that, within only a few years from now, most mobile telephony operators, at least in the world's more advanced mobile markets, will have an all-you-can-eat music service as a

part of their consumer proposition. Whether the uptake among mobile telephony subscribers will stay in the 3 per cent range, as in the SK Telecom/MelOn case, or if these bundles will be able to satisfy a greater portion of the consumers' music demand remains to be seen. It is also interesting to ponder whether this model may be able to offer on-demand access to other information products such as movies, videogames, TV series and audiobooks. The future will tell.

To service, or not to service
Although there are several exciting business models being tested in the market, the elephant is still in the room. I argue in this book that rights holders in the new music economy are unable to control the digital distribution of their intellectual properties. As soon as some kind of information is uploaded to the Cloud, it is instantly universally accessible to everyone connected. As previously reasoned, in such a friction-free network, the commercial value of providing access to individual tracks is fairly close to zero. Hence, it is possible to conclude that some of the business models presented above have a relatively bleak future while others have better sustainability. While I believe it will be increasingly difficult to convince music listeners to pay for individual tracks, I also believe, and hope, that different versions of the all-you-can-eat streaming service will be important components of the new music economy. As was discussed above, such services are possible to bundle with other kinds of media and communication services, they can be financed through various combinations of adverts and subscriptions, and they can easily be offered as different versions offering different kinds of add-on features. At the time of writing there already are several entrepreneurs ready to launch such services. The problem is that the rights holders are holding the services back since they fear that they will cannibalize their existing businesses. Certainly, their fears are understandable since these services probably *will* cannibalize their existing businesses. The dilemma is shared by players in many other copyright industries: clearly, the trick

in media's brave new world is to structure emerging distribution modes so that they are additive, not cannibalistic, to new and existing content exhibition windows, while providing new venues for advertisers (Mermigas 2006).

Surely such an ambition is understandable, but it is also associated with a high level of risk. By applying this relatively defensive strategy, as suggested by Mermigas, the firm runs the risk of being unable to respond to major shifts in their environment, such as the one currently at hand (Miles & Snow 1978). A more appropriate adaptation strategy is the *prospector* approach where innovation is of highest priority. In a copyright industry such as this one, the prospector is a far more sustainable strategy, although it, in the short term, may yield lower profit levels than the *defender* strategy.

Since the traditional recorded music business is rapidly disappearing, record labels hopefully will change their stance and embrace the new music economy once and for all. There are inspiring examples from other firms which have been able to renew themselves, turn back the industry lifecycle to an earlier stage and continue their existence for several years forward. IBM is one such company which has been able to renew its business more than once during its century-long history. Lou Gerstner, the CEO who turned IBM around during the 1990s, explained their problems:

> The company didn't lack for smart, talented people. It had file drawers full of winning strategies. Yet the company was frozen in place (p. 16) . . . all of these capabilities were part of a business model that had fallen wildly out of step with marketplace realities (p. 176) . . .History shows that the truly great and successful companies go through constant and sometimes difficult self-renewal of the base business (p. 220). (Gerstner 2002)

One lesson to be learnt from the IBM case is how important it is for firms to be able to 'unfreeze' their traditional way of thinking and challenge the truths that for too long have been taken for granted. Such soul-searching is a challenging process to get through, but one which the recorded music business has to recording. In the beginning of their careers, they recorded their music live to mono or to two-track recorders, but in the mid-1960s both bands got access to multi-track recorders which enabled them to develop entirely new sounds and arrangements. The pioneering sounds of The Beach Boys' album *Pet Sounds* and The Beatles' album *Sgt Pepper's Lonely Hearts Club Band* were enabled by multi-track recorders. For both bands, there are certain individuals who have been recognized as very influential creative and technical forces behind the sound – the producers. In the case of The Beach Boys, the producer was Brian Wilson; and in the case of The Beatles, it was George Martin. Brian Wilson was a member of the band but he also had the role of composer, arranger and studio engineer. George Martin was not formally a member of The Beatles, but he was so intimately involved in creating the band's sound that he is often recognized as the 'fifth Beatle'. Multi-track recording technology contributed enormously to the shaping of the modern role of the music producer, which today includes facets such as composing, A&R and hands-on work at the mixer console.

Digital audio-recording technologies have continued the shaping of the role and practice of the music producer. Digital technologies make it possible to sample, loop and process sounds into completely new songs, arrangements and musical genres, and the gradual shift of the locus of the creative work – from the studio to the control room – has continued and accelerated. One important aspect of digital audio-recording technologies is their ability to compensate for 'mistakes' made by musicians and singers. For instance, a couple of tones slightly out-of-pitch are no problem at all with modern pitch-correction software, which is able to make even the most tone-deaf singer seem to have perfect pitch. With digital audio-recording, it is possible to create the 'perfect' sound, with perfect pitch, perfect tempo and perfect timbre, even though the artistic raw material might not be very musically gifted.

In some genres, the music producer is the single creative force behind the musical output, and the artist has more or less

pass, if it does not want to be reduced to an entry in the history books.

In this chapter I have looked at how the music business interplays with the media and how digital technologies transform that relationship. I have discussed how the industry's centre of gravity has moved away from recorded music towards other parts of the industry. I have also discussed a number of potential revenue models which might be able to work as the basis for profitable online-based recorded music businesses.

4

Making Music

In this chapter I focus on how the professional making of music takes place in the new music economy. I look at how the ways creative people define their occupations and organize their careers can influence the nature of the work they produce. I explore the concept of the artist as a brand and link that discussion to the changing practices and routines related to talent development. I analyse developments within the live music area and discuss how the contractual relationships between artists and their business partners are affected by the new music industry dynamics.

Professions and practices

One of the most important characteristics of the new music economy is the ability for amateurs to express their creativity by making and publishing music in the Cloud. The distance between the amateur and the professional artist has been radically reduced. Even though content generated by users may be important to music firms, every teenager yearning for a place in the limelight will not succeed. The combination of drive, talent and luck simply is not homogeneously distributed across the population. In the end, only an extremely small number of people will be able to make a decent living as a creative force in the music industry. But a very interesting question is what does it mean to be a professional artist, songwriter etc.? Is it even possible to claim that such activities are professions? These kinds of questions have been discussed by several popular music scholars, for instance by Jason Toynbee (2000). It is clear that during the decades when the music industry has entered the digital age,

a powerful process of reprofessionalization has also taken place. One of the professions that has most fundamentally been redefined is that of the music producer.

The music producer

Prior to the 1950s, music recording was a well-structured process which was carried out by people with a number of equally well-defined roles. A&R agents 'discovered' the potential talent and signed them to the label; songwriters provided the artist with new material; and the in-house studio engineers controlled the machinery and ensured the sound met the expectations of the creatives and the marketers. During the 1950s and 1960s, this structure was challenged when a new technology entered the recording studios. This new technology, which is referred to as multi-track recording, is one of the most revolutionary audio-recording innovations (Cunningham 1999; Moorefield 2005).

Before multi-track recording, musicians and singers delivered their songs as a live band and had to make sure that it sounded at least good enough to be pressed to plastic. When someone played the wrong note or made some other kind of 'mistake', the entire song had to be re-recorded or the mistake had to be accepted as a creative interpretation of the song. Multi-track recorders changed this production process entirely since they enabled the recording of *individual* instruments and voices, rather than all instruments and voices at the same time. If there was a mistake in one of the channels, that specific channel could be re-recorded without affecting all the others. Multi-track recording also made it possible to change the song quite radically, even after all the musicians and singers had left the studio. For instance, the level of voices or instruments could be changed, or specific voices and instruments could be moved around within the stereophonic audio space. In other words, multi-track recorders moved some of the creative work from the studio into the control room and into the hands of the studio engineer or the *music producer*.

The Beach Boys and The Beatles were two acts which stood in the centre of the transformation from mono to multi-track been removed from the creative process. This new situation opens up fresh opportunities for the music producer with an entrepreneurial mind. One option is to cooperate with an artist who might not have the best musical abilities but who has an image and visual appearance which are able to connect with the target audience's expectations and desires. One relatively early production team following this strategy was the UK-based Stock, Aitken and Waterman who, during the 1980s and 1990s, produced a string of hits together with acts such as Bananarama, Rick Astley, Kylie Minogue, Jason Donovan, Samantha Fox and many others (Stock 2004). Some years later, a similar model was used by several members of the Swedish music producer community. One example is the music producer team linked to Cheiron Studios in Stockholm, Sweden. Cheiron Studios was founded by Denniz Pop and Tom Talomma in 1992. Later they were joined by talented producers such as Andreas Carlsson, Jörgen Elofsson, Max Martin and others. These producers have provided their services to artists such as Britney Spears, Westlife, N'Sync, Backstreet Boys, Céline Dion and Bon Jovi. Even though Max Martin and friends may be superstars within the international music producer community, none of them have desired or managed to create a mainstream recognition which is able to compete with the fame and recognition of their superstar partners. However, there are other music producers who have taken the development of their role full circle by eliminating the artist altogether and entering the limelight themselves. For instance, there are a number of US-based music producers, especially within the R&B and hip-hop genres, who have chosen this strategy. Some of the most successful producers in this area are Dr Dre, Timbaland, Pharrell Williams and Jay-Z. Even though these producers have been able to build their careers independently from traditional artists, many of them still collaborate with singers and musicians in various projects. This collaboration is often quite different from the traditional artist–producer relationship. Sometimes the producer is promoted as the 'host' who invites artists to be featured in different songs. In other projects the artist has a more central role, but still the producer is not in any way hidden in the studio as was always the case in the old days, and he or she is consciously used and exposed together with the artist in music videos, promotional appearances and sometimes even live stage performances.

To conclude, the role of the music producer has, during the last fifty years, been transformed from engineer to stage performer. To a large extent, this transformation has been enabled, or perhaps even determined, by various technological innovations. Audio-recording technology has become increasingly tolerant of singers' and musicians' human slips, and I have now reached a state where these traditional craftsmen's competences are no longer needed to create polished, flawless, recordings. This development has so far been limited to some specific genres, and the question remains whether it ever will become the modus operandi for all kinds of music production and recording. I believe that music without flaws runs the risk of becoming lifeless and a bit boring. There are technologies which try to replicate human imperfections in order to make the music more lifelike, but still some musics and sounds *have* to be performed by human beings of flesh and blood for it to be bearable to listen to them. For instance, I would say that it is unlikely that the magical sounds and unique creativity of Wynton Marsalis, Michael 'Flea' Balzary, Polly Jean Harvey and their peers will ever be replicated by digital machinery.

Recording studio decline
Digital and analogue recording technologies have not only shaped the role of music producers but also affected their workplaces: the recording studios. In the early days of recorded music, the studio was a vital and almost defining part of the record company but parallel to the development of the music producer, independent recording studios and production companies began to emerge. However, to set up and run these professional recording studios was a fairly capital-intensive endeavour. The physical characteristics and features of the studios had to provide excellent acoustics;

4

Making Music

In this chapter I focus on how the professional making of music takes place in the new music economy. I look at how the ways creative people define their occupations and organize their careers can influence the nature of the work they produce. I explore the concept of the artist as a brand and link that discussion to the changing practices and routines related to talent development. I analyse developments within the live music area and discuss how the contractual relationships between artists and their business partners are affected by the new music industry dynamics.

Professions and practices

One of the most important characteristics of the new music economy is the ability for amateurs to express their creativity by making and publishing music in the Cloud. The distance between the amateur and the professional artist has been radically reduced. Even though content generated by users may be important to music firms, every teenager yearning for a place in the limelight will not succeed. The combination of drive, talent and luck simply is not homogeneously distributed across the population. In the end, only an extremely small number of people will be able to make a decent living as a creative force in the music industry. But a very interesting question is what does it mean to be a professional artist, songwriter etc.? Is it even possible to claim that such activities are professions? These kinds of questions have been discussed by several popular music scholars, for instance by Jason Toynbee (2000). It is clear that during the decades when the music industry has entered the digital age, pass, if it does not want to be reduced to an entry in the history books.

In this chapter I have looked at how the music business interplays with the media and how digital technologies transform that relationship. I have discussed how the industry's centre of gravity has moved away from recorded music towards other parts of the industry. I have also discussed a number of potential revenue models which might be able to work as the basis for profitable online-based recorded music businesses.

recording. In the beginning of their careers, they recorded their music live to mono or to two-track recorders, but in the mid-1960s both bands got access to multi-track recorders which enabled them to develop entirely new sounds and arrangements. The pioneering sounds of The Beach Boys' album *Pet Sounds* and The Beatles' album *Sgt Pepper's Lonely Hearts Club Band* were enabled by multi-track recorders. For both bands, there are certain individuals who have been recognized as very influential creative and technical forces behind the sound – the producers. In the case of The Beach Boys, the producer was Brian Wilson; and in the case of The Beatles, it was George Martin. Brian Wilson was a member of the band but he also had the role of composer, arranger and studio engineer. George Martin was not formally a member of The Beatles, but he was so intimately involved in creating the band's sound that he is often recognized as the 'fifth Beatle'. Multi-track recording technology contributed enormously to the shaping of the modern role of the music producer, which today includes facets such as composing, A&R and hands-on work at the mixer console.

Digital audio-recording technologies have continued the shaping of the role and practice of the music producer. Digital technologies make it possible to sample, loop and process sounds into completely new songs, arrangements and musical genres, and the gradual shift of the locus of the creative work – from the studio to the control room – has continued and accelerated. One important aspect of digital audio-recording technologies is their ability to compensate for 'mistakes' made by musicians and singers. For instance, a couple of tones slightly out-of-pitch are no problem at all with modern pitch-correction software, which is able to make even the most tone-deaf singer seem to have perfect pitch. With digital audio-recording, it is possible to create the 'perfect' sound, with perfect pitch, perfect tempo and perfect timbre, even though the artistic raw material might not be very musically gifted.

In some genres, the music producer is the single creative force behind the musical output, and the artist has more or less a powerful process of reprofessionalization has also taken place. One of the professions that has most fundamentally been redefined is that of the music producer.

The music producer
Prior to the 1950s, music recording was a well-structured process which was carried out by people with a number of equally well-defined roles. A&R agents 'discovered' the potential talent and signed them to the label; songwriters provided the artist with new material; and the in-house studio engineers controlled the machinery and ensured the sound met the expectations of the creatives and the marketers. During the 1950s and 1960s, this structure was challenged when a new technology entered the recording studios. This new technology, which is referred to as multi-track recording, is one of the most revolutionary audio-recording innovations (Cunningham 1999; Moorefield 2005).

Before multi-track recording, musicians and singers delivered their songs as a live band and had to make sure that it sounded at least good enough to be pressed to plastic. When someone played the wrong note or made some other kind of 'mistake', the entire song had to be re-recorded or the mistake had to be accepted as a creative interpretation of the song. Multi-track recorders changed this production process entirely since they enabled the recording of *individual* instruments and voices, rather than all instruments and voices at the same time. If there was a mistake in one of the channels, that specific channel could be re-recorded without affecting all the others. Multi-track recording also made it possible to change the song quite radically, even after all the musicians and singers had left the studio. For instance, the level of voices or instruments could be changed, or specific voices and instruments could be moved around within the stereophonic audio space. In other words, multi-track recorders moved some of the creative work from the studio into the control room and into the hands of the studio engineer or the *music producer*.

The Beach Boys and The Beatles were two acts which stood in the centre of the transformation from mono to multi-track the facilities had to be pleasant enough to ensure that artists get inspired or simply had somewhere to hang out while waiting for the next take; the recording equipment required major investments and continuous reinvestments in order to be up-to-date with the latest technological development. Consequently, most artists were unable to have their own professional music studio in their basement. When there was a recording project underway, they simply had to turn to the recording studio and pay an hourly or daily fee to get access to the studio facilities and equipment. The continuous and steady production of records meant that the established studios had an equally steady and predictable demand for their services. Times were good (Cunningham 1999).

However, during the 1980s and 1990s, the steady situation changed as digital recording technologies dramatically lowered the costs of tools and equipment for music recording. Expensive mixing consoles, tape recorders and other tools required for analogue recording were replaced by digital equivalents which could be bought for a fraction of the cost of their analogue ancestors. This development has continued and, by the end of the first decade of the new millennium, most of the tools required to produce a professional recording are software-based and can fit into ordinary laptop computers. As a consequence, most artists and musicians can afford to have their own complete and professional recording studio in their living room. This new competition from small digital studios has made life difficult for many traditional studios, and even legendary recording studios like The Hit Factory in New York City have been forced out of business (Bukowsky & Connor 2005). However, there seems still to be a demand for some studio services. One example of a studio which has been able to enter the digital music business successfully is the renowned Abbey Road Studios in London, UK. A combination of skilled engineers, first-rate facilities and a decent history has enabled Abbey Road Studios to remain relevant not only for recording large classical music orchestras but also for smaller popular music projects. A completely different studio strategy is to focus less on tools and facilities and more on providing a unique environment to stimulate the artists' creativity. One rather unorthodox studio which has followed this path is Silence Studio in Koppom (pop. 633), Sweden – far away from every global music metropolis. Silence competes with urban studios by being as different as possible. As suggested by the name, the studio location allows artists to be immersed in the light, sounds and ambience of the peaceful Nordic natural environment and thereby to reach entirely new creative spheres. One interesting question raised by phenomena such as Silence is whether digital technologies may reduce the importance of being close to music business decision-makers in New York, Los Angeles and London – a question which will be explored in the next section.

Music production and geography
When the music business is in the Cloud, the production of music is almost entirely disconnected from the physical geography. Above I discussed how the development of new tools for music recording has driven major recording studios out of business. Popular music producers no longer have to pay expensive rents to get access to recording facilities but are able to make high-quality recordings in their living room by the use of a laptop computer and a couple of decent condenser microphones. In addition, the Internet makes it possible for the artists, musicians and technicians working together on a recording to be located in entirely different locations of the world. For instance, some instrument may be recorded in Berlin, then it is sent to New Delhi, where a talented sitar player adds a solo to the track, and finally the mastering is made in a studio in Sãu Paulo, Brazil.

Based on this reasoning, one might assume that if you want a career in the Cloud-based music business, it is possible to stay in Snohomish and you no longer have to move to New York or to Tokyo. However, that is not entirely true. Surely it may be possible to sustain a living as an expert in some area and live geographically disconnected from your fellow co-workers. However, research has shown that geography does matter, and the established geographical nodes in the world of music most likely will continue to play important roles in the global music industrial system of the future.

This kind of research is largely based on Michael Porter's work on cluster dynamics during the 1990s. In a number of significant publications (e.g. 1990; 1991) Porter explained how the success of companies is influenced by geographical conditions. Porter's model summarizes a number of factors which determine whether a certain geographical area is good for business or not. The factors in the model constitute a dynamic system which requires considerable time to develop, but if the circumstances are right, a reinforcing feedback loop may be established which may create considerable competitive advantages. The model has been used by economic geographers in the analysis of various national and regional economies. It has also been used to analyse the copyright and cultural industries linked to such regions. Hallencreutz and Power have been influenced by Porter's thinking about regions as dynamic systems and have applied the model to the Nordic music industries (Hallencreutz 2002; Power 2003) and to Swedish copyright industries in general (Power 2002).

This body of research is able to explain how clusters such as Kingston, Jamaica, or Stockholm, Sweden, have been established. They show that the physical proximity remains important even though the recording of music may be more or less disconnected from the geography. One explanation of the lingering importance of physical space in the music business is of course that recording is merely one part of the music system. Live music is perhaps even more important to the growth and sustainment of a musical cluster than recorded music, and, of course, live music remains as a non-digitizable real world phenomenon. In addition, many other factors of the music industrial cluster remain linked to the physical world. Music is an inherently communal experience, not only on stage, but also during practising and learning. In order to grow as a musician, it is necessary to meet, play and interact with other musicians, something which preferably occurs in real life.

Talent development

The change of the music producer's profession along with the change of the structure of the music production system is one important aspect of making music in the Cloud. The new recording technologies and practices have caused the overall costs of making a recording to collapse. However, in a world where information is abundant and attention is scarce, the costs of getting that attention have moved in the opposite direction. The music firm's marketing budget for an album project is usually set as a percentage of expected sales. Previously this percentage hovered around 10 per cent, but the changes in the media environment have forced many music firms to let their marketing budgets climb closer to 20 per cent. A marketing director at a major label explains their thinking related to traditional television advertising: 'We have accustomed the consumer to music adverts which has created a situation where more TV spots are required to get the consumer to the record store. Today you need maybe five to ten spots when it previously was enough with less than five.'

However, the actual size of the marketing budgets exhibits an interesting dynamics due to its dependence on album sales. After having increased in absolute numbers during the 1990s, when the sales of recorded music plummeted during the first decade of the twenty-first century, marketing budgets shrank along with them. This change is especially visible in relation to music video production. The use of moving images to promote music can be traced back to the 1960s (Bob Dylan, The Monkees, The Beatles et al.) and the 1970s (David Bowie, ABBA, Queen et al.) but the definitive milestone is the launch of MTV in the US on 1 August 1981 (Denisoff 1988:37). MTV established a new platform for music promotion and spurred the music firms' marketing departments to spend a growing portion of their marketing budgets on the production of promotional videos. This portion expanded due to the assumption that, in order to reach the audience, the video had to beat the extravagance of the competition. The assumption established a reinforcing feedback process which rapidly accelerated music video production costs, and eventually peaked in 1995 with Michael and Janet Jackson's *Scream*, directed by Mark Romanek, and often cited as the most expensive music video ever made. Now, due to the reduced sales of recorded music, the music video production budgets have been considerably reduced, and, also, fewer songs are supported by a promotional video. A former product manager at a major label explains:

> when I started in the music business . . . I had in the beginning I would say for an average music video up to €150,000. When I left [a multinational music firm] in 2003 I had something like a rule that said €50,000 maximum. . . .You could feel that the budgets definitely had been reduced . . . we had to get the same media awareness and same media volume for less budget . . . we just didn't have the budgets to work with artists that weren't priority artists, key artists [that] I were hoping to exploit in other territories.

The pattern of behaviour created by the music firms' promotional strategies can be summarized as follows: the transformation of the media environment initially forced music firms to increase their marketing effort and budgets to uphold their media presence. At first, the audience–media engine continued to run fairly well, but as the media environment continued to evolve, the music firms eventually were unable to follow the evolution by continuously increasing their marketing effort. Consequently, the music firms pulled the brakes and revised their strategies again. This time, marketing effort was reduced, but the marketing resources were not evenly distributed across the entire artist roster. The firms' marketing efforts were instead focused on a limited set of prioritized artists, based on the understanding that you have to focus your resources to be heard through the media noise. The prioritized artists required a wide audience appeal in order to be able to recoup the marketing costs. Consequently, artists in the major music firm's roster with a narrow audience appeal were often less fortunate when competing for the firm's attention and resources.

As fewer artists in the roster get access to the music firm's marketing support, it makes no sense to keep unsupported artists. An A&R agent at a major describes his view on the change: 'seven years ago I would have hundreds of artists that I weren't able to give 100 percent . . . but now when I have reduced the number of artists in the roster, I feel that I are able to pay more attention to every single artist'.

During the last couple of years, record labels' artist rosters have been significantly reduced. Artists with a broad audience appeal have been prioritized before artists with niche appeal since artists of the former category are more likely to recoup the firm's investment in production and marketing. EMI explain their version of this strategy in a press release from March 2004: 'EMI is reducing its global roster by approximately 20 percent, affecting largely niche and under-performing artists. The roster is being rebalanced to focus resources and efforts more effectively on the artists who have the greatest potential on both a global and local level' (EMI 2004). Following the same reasoning, music firms have grown less patient with their artists. Artists have to be continuously profitable; otherwise they will be dropped from the roster. One classic example of an artist who was unable to create continuously profitable albums is the R&B singer Mariah Carey. During 2001 Carey was signed to EMI, but when her album *Glitter* 'only' sold about 500,000 units, the label decided to terminate their contract with the artist (EMI 2002b).

The increased pressure affects not only the labels' relationships with seasoned artists but also their relationships with less experienced talents. Previously a new artist signed to a major record label was able to learn and evolve during at least two full-length albums. Now, the demands on the new talents have changed quite considerably. Never has the old adage 'you are only as good as your last recording' ever been more true than today. The A&R agent quoted above reflects on the situation:

> the executives I play our music for . . . when I bring in something that I love . . . they just ask 'where is the hit, where is the single?', they don't want to hear 'this is a great act, let's put them on the road for two years and see what happens', they want to hear which is the radio song and what is the immediate plan to gain them some audience . . . it used to be . . . you can build an artist's career, you might have three albums with that one artist . . . if the first album is not successful you have the second album and the third album . . . now if the first album is not successful, the artist is probably going to be dropped. You have fewer chances with your artist to make it and to become successful . . . it's got to be now . . . everything is very immediate.

While it may be regrettable that so many major artists are now without contracts it is even more frightening that the major music firms seem to be no longer interested in developing new talent. As an executive explained to us regarding the chances of a new artist to remain on the label, 'one shot and that's it, there are no second chances in this business anymore'. Another informant continued: 'We are signing less number of acts per year, than I probably were, because I don't have the same amount of money as I used to . . . We definitely look for artists that have built up their fan base already and have experience, because first and foremost, you get better with every show . . . yes I definitely want more seasoned road warriors to say the least.'

This change of policy could be described as if the record labels outsource the talent development activity completely. As I noted earlier, for a number of years, smaller independent record labels have been acting as the research and development departments of the music industry (see e.g. Wallis 1995). Smaller labels have often developed new artists or genres which, when they have reached commercial success, have been acquired by a major. Either the major has acquired the independent label in full or it has bought out a specific artist in the indie label's roster. During recent years this routine has been developed further by majors in the shape of 'upstream deals' signed with the independent labels. An A&R director at a New York-based music publisher:

> [the labels] turn to not wanting to do any of the artist development themselves . . . labels are now signing production deals with producers and independent labels . . . every label wants to do what they call upstream deals . . . where they sign an independent label and if it is a rock band they'll let it go in this little indie label first . . . the indie label develops it . . . if it sells 50,000 or 100,000 units it gets upstreamed to the major . . . and that is how a lot of different artists are working these days . . . they don't want to spend the money on studio time as they used to . . . they don't want to give advances to producers just to develop an artist even when they need to grow . . . maybe on their second record . . . the labels are not taking those chances anymore.

The reasoning in this section shows how the major labels are affected by the new music economy. I have shown that as costs of marketing climb, labels retreat from the most important components of music business – signing and developing new talents.

The artist as a brand

One way of dealing with the rising costs of getting and keeping attention in the new music economy is to treat artists and bands like brands (see e.g. Kapferer 2004). It is very costly to establish a new brand. First, the audience has to learn about the existence of the brand, and then the audience has to attach the right values to the brand in question. These processes are usually both expensive and difficult, regardless of industry or product.

It is possible to look at music firms' reluctance to sign new and unproven talents from a brand-management perspective. Basically, since it is costly to develop new brands it makes sense, from a brand-management perspective, to invest in already established brands, or to build low-risk brands which are able to survive for decades. I shall look into two manifestations of these strategies next.

Table 4.1 The average age of top-10 global superstars	
Period	*Average age*
1989–1991	36 yrs
1995–1997	42 yrs
2001–2003	45 yrs
2004–2007	48 yrs

Ageing superstars

One way to illustrate music firms' reluctance to invest in new and unproven talent may be to look at how the age of the highest-earning artists during a given year has developed. An analysis based on data published in *Forbes*, *Rolling Stone* and *Billboard* show that, in 1990, the average age of the top-10 global superstars was thirty-six. Around 2006, the average age was forty-eight (table 4.1).

Following the reasoning to music firms' investments in old and new talents, the explanation for the increasing average age of the superstar would be that there is simply not enough new talent being developed to feed the superstar system. However, there could of course be another explanation to the trend. The consumers, the rockers of the 1960s, are growing old together with their life-long idols. Not only have these consumers a conservative and unchanging music taste, they also have quite a lot of money, compared to teenagers – at least which they are willing to spend on music. While this is happening, the kids spend less and less on music, which in combination transforms music into a geriatric rather than a pubertal vocation.

A somewhat morbid extension of the trend of the ageing superstar is that some of the most profitable music brands are related to artists who actually have passed away. The *Forbes* (2007) annual list of the Top-Earning Dead Celebrities showed that they grossed a combined $232 million in 2006. Indeed, all the members of this elite club are the lynchpins of enormously profitable – and growing – merchandising empires. Dead musicians make up a majority of the list due to the music industry's unique royalty system.

In death, there can only be one King of music, Elvis Presley, whose estate generated $49 million in 2006. CKX Entertainment, the publicly traded firm which presides over the bulk of the Elvis empire (daughter Lisa Marie Presley retains a 15-per cent stake) announced a massive overhaul of Graceland, marking the thirtieth anniversary of the 15 King's death. Revenues from Graceland were up 15 per cent in 2006, to $35 million. And that doesn't include royalties generated from Elvis music, DVDs and licensing deals like the one struck with Cirque du Soleil for an Elvis-themed revue in Las Vegas.

John Lennon is listed in second place, with earnings estimated at $44 million. In February 2006, the Beatles settled a fifteen-year battle with Apple (the computer company) over the company's decision to get into the music business. (The Beatles' commercial interests are overseen by a firm called Apple Corps.) Two months later, the band settled another long-standing dispute with its record label EMI over alleged unpaid royalties. The settlements, which are believed to have exceeded $100 million, also buoyed the income of the other deceased Beatle, George Harrison, who placed number three on the list, with earnings estimated at $22 million.

Tupac Shakur is fourth on the list with $9 million. Over a decade after his unsolved 1996 murder in a drive-by shooting, Tupac remains a hot commercial property. Said to be in development are a Tupac biopic, a videogame and a Broadway show. James Brown is number five on the list. When he died on Christmas Day 2006, the 'Godfather of Soul' left behind a probate nightmare – an out-of-date will, a recent marriage and a handful of alleged heirs claiming Brown was their father. At stake are royalties from a vast music portfolio that includes iconic singles like 'Papa's Got a Brand New Bag', 'I Got You (I Feel Good)' and 'Please, Please, Please'.

Number six on the list is Bob Marley. Fifty-Six Hope Road, which manages the Rastafarian superstar's music on behalf of the Marley family, enjoys royalties from the Marley catalogue, including *Legend*, the bestselling reggae album in history. The family, which also sells Marley-branded apparel and paraphernalia online, is pursuing legal action against Universal Music (which owns rights to some of Marley's biggest hits) and Verizon Wireless for allegedly selling Marley ringtones without permission. While royalties have long been a staple source of income for the Top-Earning Dead Celebrities, who collects them has now become a hotly debated issue in the entertainment community.

Manufactured music brands
The second brand-management strategy commonly used in the music industry is to create brands which are disconnected from an artist of flesh and blood. It could for instance be a connection to a media brand (e.g. a videogame, a radio station, a film or a TV series); a genre (e.g. jazz, garage rock, opera or reggaeton); a certain activity or mood (e.g. relaxation, depression, pregnancy or workout); a time period (e.g. hits from the 1980s); a specific season (e.g. Christmas songs or summer songs); a specific record label (e.g. Sun Records; Motown Records); or simply a collection of recent hits.

There are at least two parties involved in these kinds of projects: the owner of the brand and the owner of the musical content. The rationale behind these projects differs between brand owner and content owner. The brand owner does not necessarily have to be part of the music industry, but might be any kind of consumer-oriented firm. For instance, the clothing manufacturer Levi Strauss & Co. has released a number of albums which include some of the songs licensed for use in their commercials.

It is very rational from a brand-management perspective to work with brands such as 'Pop Idol' or 'High School Musical' rather than with traditional artist brands. Traditional artist brands such as 'Amy Winehouse' or 'Velvet Revolver' are considered to be successful if they are able to create four or five profitable albums during their career. This should be contrasted with 'manufactured' music brands which, if managed well, can go on forever. The 'Now that's what I call music' compilation series has for instance released 211 albums between 1983 and 2006, primarily in the UK but also in other markets around the world (http://www.nowmusic.com). Another similar brand, 'Absolute', has released 220 albums between 1986 and 2006 in Sweden only. During 2005, every tenth album sold in Sweden was an 'Absolute' album (http://www.absolute.se). This arithmetic shows quite bluntly why it is much more appealing, from a business perspective, to establish such a manufactured music brand compared to a traditional one. In addition, manufactured music brands are in less need of promotion tours and radio airplay, they never get old and never have to spend time on drug rehabilitation programmes (Wikström & Burnett 2009).

Pop Idol

In relation to the sections on music brands and talent development it is relevant to point to a media phenomenon which became extremely successful during the first decade of this century, namely the televised talent shows, where Freemantle Media's *Pop Idol*[26] franchise has risen as the victor. *Pop Idol* is an unscripted TV show which invites hopeful amateur singers to audition for the programme. From the thousands of applicants, a jury chooses between ten and fifteen singing talents who become part of the interactive live show which runs for a number of episodes throughout a season. During each episode the Idols give a performance which is followed by often harsh criticism from the jury. The television viewers are then supposed to vote by telephone or mobile phone texting for their favourite participant. At the end of each episode the participant who has received the least number of votes has to leave the show. *Pop Idol* has been commissioned and produced in forty territories around the world and at the time of writing more than 3 billion telephony votes have been cast by viewers around the world since the launch of the programme in the UK in 2001. Participants who remain in the show until the end of the season are offered a studio recording contract and possibly also marketing support by the participating music firm (usually Sony Music). An album is released immediately after the final episode, and, so far, the media presence stirred by the show has been able to bring every winner's album immediately to the top tier of the nation's weekly chart (http://www.freemantlemedia.com).

Some of the talents scouted during these shows, for instance Kelly Clarkson, Chris Daughtry, Darin Zanyar, Danny Saucedo, Will Young, Mark Medlock and many others, have had a strong development of their careers. For instance, Kelly Clarkson (US) was the winner of *American Idol* in 2002. The three albums[27] since her *Pop Idol* appearance have all been commercial successes and the second album received two US Grammy awards in February 2006. Clarkson is also the only Idol personality who has been able to expand her brand recognition beyond the national borders. Other successful *Pop Idol* talents are Darin Zanyar from Sweden and Will Young from the UK; both have been able to launch careers that span more than one album. Young has received several Brit Awards and Zanyar received a Swedish Grammy in February 2006. However, neither Young nor Zanyar has been able to take the step from national recognition to international stardom (http://www.bpi.co.uk; http://www.riaa.org; http://www.ifpi.se).

As with most unscripted television shows, the *Idol* series are not particularly well respected by artists with 'cred' or by the cultural elite (see e.g. Hansson 2004; *Svenska Dagbladet* 2004). However, still after several seasons, the shows receive high ratings in most territories where it has been licensed and it continues to make good economic sense to the parties involved. Broadcasters are happy since the format attracts an audience that advertisers are willing to purchase. Music firms are also happy since they are able to find talented personalities. Most importantly, the audience–media engine is kick-started since these personalities become well known among the mainstream audience *before* the actual start of their musical careers.

It is reasonable to expect that media brands which are not immediately linked to a specific music personality of flesh and blood will become more common in the new music economy.

There are already a number of successful brands of this kind, for instance 'The Gorillaz' or 'The Pussycat Dolls'. The 'members' of 'The Gorillaz' are computer-animated characters and, in the case of 'The Pussycat Dolls', the members of the group are merely salaried employees of the record label Interscope and hence completely interchangeable (*The Irish Times* 2006). According to such music industry logic, the performers may still be the face of a project but they are no longer the 'stars'. Rather, the star is the producer or perhaps the entire creative team who is managing and controlling the shape and content of the music brand.

Live music

The music industry during the last century has primarily been dominated by the record companies' values and perspectives. Most other parts of the music industry, including live music, have primarily been considered as means to promote the industry's most important product, i.e. the recording. However, during recent decades the balance between live music and recorded music has shifted. While the sales of recorded music have diminished during the last decade, the revenues from live music are rapidly growing.

There are at least two ways to explain the growth of the live music sector. First, the average price of concert tickets has increased, and second, more artists are giving more concerts which have caused the number of shows to multiply. Let us look into each of these two observations.

The average price of concert tickets has increased significantly more than the average inflation rate during the last decade. It is difficult to explain the increase in ticket prices simply by pointing to increasing production costs. Certainly, the live music industry is an industry with relatively slow productivity growth, and in such industries prices are due to the increasing costs, which are expected to grow faster than the overall inflation. However, this reasoning is unable to explain the sudden change of the growth rate of concert ticket prices at the end of the 1990s. A more plausible explanation of that pattern is related to the performers and their demand for higher guaranteed payment levels. The performers' push for higher guarantees is understandable in the light of the falling revenues from recorded music. By increasing the guarantees and as a consequence the ticket prices, it is possible at least to some extent to compensate for the reduced income from recorded music.

The loss of revenue from recorded music is also able to explain the increase in the number of events. For obvious reasons, a live music experience is difficult to digitize, and is therefore considerably easier to control compared to those areas of the industry which have been affected more profoundly by digital technologies. Artists who previously were able to earn their livelihood from recorded music have greater and greater difficulties sustaining their businesses. As a consequence, more and more artists resort to touring, which has caused the number of yearly concert events to grow.

The changing purpose and position of the live music sector
The increasing revenues from live music in combination with the decreasing revenues from recorded music have changed the purpose and position of live concerts in the music industry. In the good old days, live music and touring were the way to promote an artist and to increase the demand for the artist's recordings. Typically, a record was made, and a tour was launched to support the sales of that record. It was of less importance whether the tour was profitable or not since losses generally could be recouped from record sales. However, since the sales of music have decreased so rapidly, it is no longer possible to allow touring projects to be unprofitable. Most live music projects have to be considered as stand-alone and able to cover their own costs.

During recent years the relationship between live music and recorded music has been reversed. Rather than expecting live music to stimulate sales of recorded music, in the new music economy, recorded music is often used to stimulate ticket sales.

CASE STUDY: PRINCE'S *PLANET EARTH*

Bundling strategies have also been used in other ways in relation to the music industry, for instance when CDs are distributed as covermounts on magazines. One such project involves the R&B artist Prince's forty-sixth album *Planet Earth*. Three million copies of the album were distributed with the British newspaper *Mail on Sunday* on 15 July 2007. The initiative raised much aggravation among bricks-and-mortar retailers who called the campaign an insult to those who had supported the artist's career during three decades and blaming the artist for devaluing music. The project is indeed interesting from a bundling perspective but it also shows how the sales of recorded music have lost their position as the industry's most important revenue generator. As Prince gives away the recorded music for free, he maximizes the reach of his music in order to promote the real revenue generator: a residency at the O2 Arena in London produced by AEG Live and comprising of twenty-one shows in total. With 351,000 tickets sold at £31.21 (a reference to his previous album which was titled *3121*) the series grossed close to £11 million.

One example of such a project is Prince's *Planet Earth* project in the UK in 2007, which completely adhered to this logic.

As a result of the increased importance of live music, the actors within this industry segment have also become more influential in the general music industry. Live Nation, the global giant of the live music business, is a live events company formed in 2005 by a spin-off from Clear Channel Communication.

Live Nation launched a new business area in 2007, dubbed Live Nation Artists with the intention of bringing artists closer to the firm. The business area provides services such as merchandise development and sales, fan site operation, rights management, ticketing and recordings. By offering these services, it is possible for Live Nation to push the record label out of the equation and to take advantage of a range of revenue streams generated by the artist, not only limited to live music.

This kind of model, usually referred to as the 360-degree model, has become a more and more common phenomenon in the music industry. It was initially introduced by record labels such as Sanctuary Records in the UK, with the intention of increasing the label's share of the revenues from merchandising, licensing, touring etc. One early 360-deal which gained much attention at the time was the contract between EMI and Robbie Williams, estimated to be worth £80 million (Gibbons 2002). A consequence of the 360-degree model is that sales of recorded music become merely one in a range of other, sometimes larger, revenue streams. Hence, it is not a given that the main actor of such an agreement has to be a record label; it might as well be concert promoters such as Live Nation or even ordinary private equity firms, such as UK-based The Edge Group or Ingenious Media.

Live Nation's first high-profile deal was presented in 2007 when they were able to convince Madonna to leave Warner Music, and to sign a new $120 million contract with Live Nation Artists (Smith 2007). The deal marks a massive shift for Madonna, who has been with Warner almost her entire career, starting in 1983. The contract provides the performer with a mix of cash and stock in exchange for the rights to sell three albums, promote concert tours, sell merchandise and license her name for sponsorship deals. Madonna received a signing bonus of about $18 million and an advance of roughly $17 million for each of three albums. Another $50 million is expected to be handed out in stock and shares.

Live Nation presented another deal in April 2008, when they were able to sign Jay-Z to their growing roster (*New York Times* 2008). The contract amounted to $150 million, one of the richest contracts ever awarded to a musician. This partnership, which will be named Roc Nation, will include financing for Jay-Z's own entertainment ventures (which are expected to become a record label, talent/management agency and music-publishing company). Live Nation is expected to contribute $5 million a year in overheads for five years, with another $25 million available to finance Jay-Z's acquisitions or investments. Roc Nation would then split profits with Live Nation. To finalize the deal, Jay-Z will depart from Def Jam Records after he turns in his last required album under his talent contract.

On 31 March 2008, it was confirmed that U2 signed a twelve-year deal with Live Nation worth an estimated $100 million. The deal includes Live Nation controlling the band's merchandise, sponsoring and their official website. Other artists that recently signed with Live Nation include Nickelback and Shakira. Mainly a concert promoter, Live Nation 'signs' artists as a 'record label', but predominantly takes the role of a promoter, rather than 'owner of music'.

This all sounds very close to the description offered by Tremlett: 'The music industry is nothing more than that: An industry that makes money out of music, dealing and trading in this commodity with as much refinement as the second-hand car trade' (1990:175). Depending on the outcome of these new deals and experiments, the relationship between artist and music company might well never be the same again, thus having tremendous consequences for the future of the entire music industry. The revival of the live music sector is also one of the most important features of the new music economy. One might argue that, as the music firms' ability to control their assets in a digital format diminishes, live music soon will dominate the entire music industry in the same fashion as recorded music has done during more than half a century.

The relationship between the artist and what used to be the record label

The 360-degree model discussed above has gained lots of attention during the last couple of years. Some consider it to be the future of the music industry while others think it is extremely unwise for especially younger artists to put all their eggs in one basket. The proponents of the model are often also positive to the understanding of an artist as a brand. Based on that thinking, investments in a particular brand, i.e. an artist's career, will increase the equity of the brand, which in turn will generate revenues from sponsorships, film acting, merchandise, touring, licensing and of course from music sales. They argue further that it is reasonable that a record label that builds that brand equity also should get the returns from all revenues, not only from one or a few of them.

From the artist's point of view, it might be attractive to sign a 360-degree contract. Usually these contracts include rather hefty advances, and in addition it is very convenient only to have to deal with one company for all business-related matters. The problem is, however, that artists signing such a contract may run the risk of losing some of their creative control. In the relationship between artist and record label, there always is a trade-off between business risk and creative control. The 360 deal is placed on the very end on a spectrum where the record labels accept most of the business risk, and the artists lose most of their creative control. On this spectrum there are a variety of different contractual models which differ in terms of the balance between risk and control. I will look at some of these models next.

The contractual structure somewhat 'to the right' of the 360 deal is the traditional record label contract. In this structure, the label pays for the recording and handles the manufacturing, distribution, press and promotion. The artist gets an advance payment and a royalty percentage after all those other costs are repaid. If an album is a commercial failure and is unable to earn back the firm's expenses, no royalties will be paid to the artist. Since most album projects are unprofitable, it is not uncommon that artists live in constant debt to their record label, and if they hit a dry spell they can go broke.

In this type of contract, the label owns the copyright of the recording forever and ultimately decides if and how recordings should be distributed and promoted. This means that if an artist has made a recording which does not fit with the label's understanding of what kind of music is marketable – if label executives 'don't hear a single' (cf. the quotation on p. 129) – the recording might never be released.

One of the strongest objections to the traditional record label contract is the transfer of ownership of the copyrights from the artist to the record label. The *licence deal* is similar to the standard deal, except in this case the artist retains the copyrights and ownership of the master recording. The right to exploit that property is granted to a label for a limited period of time – usually seven years. After that, the rights to license to TV shows, commercials and the like revert to the artist. If a band has made a record itself and doesn't need creative or financial help, this model is often optimal. It allows for a more creative freedom, since you get less interference from the record company executives. The down side is that, because the label doesn't own the master, it may invest less in making the release a success.

As the music industry is evolving, the licence is becoming more common. There are several drivers behind this trend. First, the growing importance of copyrights and licensing has made artists increasingly aware of the importance of retaining the rights to their recordings. Second, in the old days, burgeoning artists tried to convince A&R agents by sending them relatively basic recordings of their creative ideas; today's artists are able to finance their own recordings, and are able to send the record labels full-fledged recordings of professional quality. Correspondingly, as has been discussed above, record labels are unwilling to invest in unproven artists. In a licensing deal, the record label reduces its risk since it can make a decision regarding a specific recording without having invested anything in advances or recording costs. If the label likes the recording it will sign the contract for that particular recording, pay an advance to the artist and begin its promotion and distribution activities. Otherwise, the artist is free to pursue his or her luck with other labels.

There are several variations of the licensing deal. One kind of variation could be to change the balance between the advances and the royalties paid by the label to the artist. This balance is not related to the creative control, but only to how the business risk is shared between label and artist. Another variation might concern what kind of services the record label should perform, whether manufacturing the physical product, physical distribution, online distribution, promotion etc.

As the new music economy has evolved, the contracts where the artist retains more of the control and the role of the record label is reduced become more and more common. A question soon arises – when does the record label cease to be a record label? In the old days, the primary role of the record label was to finance the recording and to manufacture, distribute and promote the disk. In the new music economy, artists are able to be in control of all these activities themselves. They are able to make the recording in their own studio; they can hire specific consultants and service companies which are happy to offer services such as marketing communication, online distribution and so on. There is no place for the record label in the new music economy. Some services are required, and there will certainly be a demand from artists for financing, distribution services, promotion services, tour production and so on, and perhaps these services will be provided by companies that previously referred to themselves as record labels, but the relationship between these entities and the artists will most likely never be like the twentieth-century record contract.

During most of the twentieth century, the record labels more or less ran the music industry. They were in power, they controlled the distribution resources, they retained the rights to the intellectual properties and so on. I have throughout this book shown how revenues from recorded music have diminished while revenues from the other two industry sectors – music licensing and live music – have increased. I have also shown how the services offered by record labels either no longer are in demand or are offered by more agile competitors.

In the new music economy, the record label is no longer in the driver's seat; it is the artist, or the artist/manager, who is. In the new music economy, the artist's role as an (involuntary) entrepreneur is strengthened. Rather than being contracted by a record company to perform certain services, the artist sets up a limited company and secures the necessary funding as

CASE STUDY: ROBYN CARLSSON

The career of the Swedish pop act Robyn Carlsson is a very telling story about the old and the new music economy.

1995   At the age of sixteen Robyn Carlsson releases her own songs 'You've got that something' and the breakthrough single 'Do you really want me?'. The singles are followed by the debut album *Robyn is Here*, produced by Cheiron's Max Martin and Denniz Pop.

1997   The singles 'Do you know (what it takes)?' and 'Show me love' are released in the US and reach the *Billboard* top-10.

1999   The album '*My Truth*' is released in Europe and the single 'Electric' is on heavy rotation. In the US the BMG label RCA refuses to release the album unless Robyn makes some of the songs more radio-friendly. She refuses and the record is never released in the US.

2002   The third album *Don't Stop the Music* is released by BMG. Due to continued problems with the record label, it is released only in Sweden.

2004   Robyn makes a recording of the song 'Who's that girl?' Again, the record label refuses to release the song, and instead releases 'Robyn's best' in the US.

2005   After all the problems with her business partner BMG, she is able to end the contract, and to start her own company, Konichiwa Records. Later that year, she records the album *Robyn* together with producers Klas Åhlund and Alexander Kronlund. Initially Konichiwa has considerable problems with getting the CD out in retail stores because the majors were very hesitant to include the product in their distribution machinery.

2006   Robyn wins several Swedish Grammy awards, among others the awards for Best Album, Best Female Artist and Best Composer (together with Klas Åhlund).

2007   *Robyn* is released in the UK and is well received by critics and fans.

2008   The album is released in the US. Robyn is met with rave reviews and appears on the David Letterman show. The single 'With every heartbeat' reaches the number one spot on the official UK chart and she has a sold-out tour in the UK. Robyn supports Madonna on her European 'Sticky & Sweet' tour.

Peter Swartling, her first producer from 1993, comments on her future career: 'Robyn is the ultimate artist but her future success has nothing to do with her talent and artistry. If it only would depend on that there would be no limit to how big she could get. Now it is all about how she is able to manage her resources and her distribution channels…. Today it is much more difficult to release an artist compared to four to five years ago, and it depends more than ever on external conditions.'

Sources: Yeaman 2008; Madonna.com 2008

they see fit. As in any limited company, funding may be in the shape of equity or liabilities; it may be from venture capitalists, from banks or from the stock market. The value of the company is raised through the accumulation of revenues from various activities and the intellectual assets developed by the artist. Most likely expenses also have to be paid for services, such as distribution, promotion etc. Of course, these kinds of companies existed also in the old music economy, but now they are increasingly common.

I started out this book by looking at the case of Trent Reznor and Nine Inch Nails. Reznor is one of the many artists using this model. Radiohead (case study on p. 110) is another one, and so is the Swedish pop act Robyn (case study on p. 144), with her Konichiwa Records. There are of course variations within the scope of this basic structure, ranging from the massive ventures such as Live Nation Artists, via mid-sized management firms such as ie:music[28] in London, to single-artist endeavours such as Robyn's Konichiwa Records in Stockholm.

This is a new structure of making music which radically differs from the old music economy. If the transformation continues, it might considerably lower the concentration of the production of music, which should call for an increase in the diversity of the music which is being produced (e.g. Dowd 2000; 2004).

This chapter has explored how professional music-making is transformed. I have looked at how the professions and practices within the production of music have changed; discussed how the development of new talents has been affected by the new business conditions; and explored how artists' careers increasingly are modelled as a matter of brand management. I continued with the development within the live music sector and the evolving relationship between the artist and its business partners. I discussed the 360-degree model, but also other structures for the agreements between artists and what formerly used to be the record label. Building on this analysis I envisioned a future where the creative artists and their managers take the leading role in the industry, which might lead to increased cultural diversity.

The next chapter will continue the analysis of music making, but I will leave the realm of the so-called professionals, and move on to the amateurs.

5

The Social and Creative Music Fan

Music plays an important role in many peoples' lives. It can wake you up in the morning and it can slow you down after work. It can get you in the mood for love and it can comfort your broken heart. It can connect you to your peers and separate you from conventions and older generations. However, there are some people who want to do more than simply listen to the music. They want to sing along or even play their own versions of their favourite songs; they want to share their feelings and musical experiences with their peers and the world; and they want to learn about every detail of the life of the celebrities. I have previously discussed how improved connectivity and more widely accessible upload capability have lowered the barriers to entering the media outlet market (see pp. 87ff. above). However, in the new music economy, these barriers are so low that every amateur musician and ordinary music fan is able to create, remix and publish music online.

The phenomenon where the audience not only passively consumes culture but also contributes in the production of that culture is often referred to as participatory culture (Jenkins 2006). Participatory culture is not at all restricted to music but can be seen in other cultural spheres such as the film, video-game or book arena. Thousands of blogs discuss the latest developments of the *Lord of the Rings* or the *Star Wars* franchises. Teenagers write and publish their own stories (i.e. fan-fiction) based on Harry Potter or Buffy the Vampire Slayer, thereby taking the characters into new, and at times controversial, territories. Music fans make their own music videos to their favourite song to express how the song makes them feel. While participatory culture is a trend pushed from the consumers' desire to be creative and social, there is another driving force towards the increased involvement of consumers in the provisioning and development of services. Providers of services such as banking, travel, healthcare etc. increasingly try to involve the consumer in their value-creation processes. Consumers are allowed direct access to the banking system to do stock trading, make money transfers or make invoice payments themselves. Online questionnaires allow patients to begin a process of self-diagnosis before meeting a doctor in the flesh. Again, it is the digital technologies which are facilitating this trend, and the motivation from the service providers' point of view is of course to lower their costs.

This chapter will explore the consumption of music, the role of the music fan and the relationship between the fan and the celebrity in the new music economy. I shall look at different parts of the value-creation process of the music business and how consumers are involved in the different phases. I also look at how some fans are helping promote their favourite artists. I start out with the last phase of the value chain – distribution.

Friendly sharing?

In a previous chapter I discussed connectivity–control aspects of the new music economy, and how rights holders have lost the ability to control the distribution of their intellectual properties. Perhaps the single most important technological concept which has pushed that irreversible process forward is peer-to-peer (P2P) networking. P2P networking is basically a principle for communicating and sharing resources in a computer network. It differs from the traditional computer network topology known as 'client-server networking'. In a client-server network, a single powerful computer serves the requests of a large number of less powerful computers, or clients. In such a network, communication between two clients has to pass through the server, which makes it relatively easy to monitor and control. If for instance a client in the client-server network distributes MP3 files without the rights holder's authorization; it is easy to locate that client and charge its owner with copyright infringement. In a true P2P network there exists no central server, and communication takes place directly between the computers connected to the network. In this kind of network, communication is much more difficult to police. In modern P2P networks a single music file (or any kind of digital information) is split up in several pieces and stored in a large number of computers which makes it even more difficult to determine who is responsible for the distribution of that particular file.

It should be noted that P2P networking as such is nothing suspicious or illegal. P2P concepts have been discussed within the Internet research community since 1969, when Steve Crocker brought the issue to the table (Crocker 1969). Several P2P networks have been launched since, for instance UseNet in 1979 and FidoNet in 1984. Since mainstream personal computers have become ever more potent and the bandwidth by which these computers are connected to the Internet has increased, P2P has become an increasingly useful model for Internet-based collaboration and networking. Today P2P networking is used in several entirely legal applications – primarily for media distribution but also for other purposes such as Internet telephony (Oram 2001).

Although P2P networking has a long history and many legitimate uses, when it in 1999 gained the awareness of the general public in the shape of the Napster software it became forever linked to the illegal distribution of recorded music (Alderman 2001). The Napster software spread quickly among Internet users and reached a popularity of giant proportions. This development did not go unnoticed by the major record labels, who brought the Napster creator Shawn Fanning to trial and ordered him to cease-and-desist. Fanning eventually followed that order, but once the P2P concept was known among the general public, other more sophisticated technologies soon followed.

File-sharing networks as Cloud-based music libraries

There has been, and still is, a relatively polarized debate as to whether it is the copyright infringement enabled by P2P networking and other similar technologies which has caused the downturn of the recorded music industry. Most rights holders, and the majority of the 'establishment', argue that digital technologies, such as P2P networking, enable consumers to acquire music without the owners' consent and without paying for the use of the products. These debaters focus on the fundamental aspects of property law and property owners' rights to decide how their assets should be exploited and used. According to this reasoning, illegal file-sharing has enabled consumers to reduce their purchases of recorded music through legitimate channels and to turn to free but illegal methods of acquiring music.

The second argument is primarily held by an exotic mix of apolitical Internet techies, anarchists and radical liberals. According to this reasoning, music firms actually benefit from the audience's increased access to musical content. The increased accessibility has facilitated audience action (cf. the audience–media engine) and more people will be able to discover music and broaden their musical experience, which is beneficial to the entire music industry. Based on that logic, the appropriate action by the music industry would be to support the uncontrolled circulation of copyrighted material on the Internet, rather than to try to wipe it out.

Several scholars and research firms have contributed to the debate. Research on US consumers shows a negative relationship between files downloaded and CDs purchased (Edison Media Research 2003; Ipsos-Reid 2002). Research made on European consumers also shows that the impact of online piracy on sales is negative. Forrester Research concluded that more than 40 per cent of frequent 'downloaders' buy less music now than they did before they began downloading. Indeed, 2 per cent of the 'downloaders' say they bought more CDs after they started downloading, but that is in no way able to balance the loss (Forrester Research 2003). Enders Analysis (2003) joins the choir by stating that online piracy 'cost about 35–40 percent of the reduction in the size of the global music market'.

The conclusion from these research reports indicates that there are other factors influencing sales of recorded music, besides the emergence of specific Internet technologies. This conclusion is supported by several scholars, for instance by Liebowitz (2002a; 2002b) who points to the general state of the economy and by Wikström (2005) who points to changes among the broadcast media and music firms' revised A&R strategies. Some scholars go as far as to argue that the effect of the Internet technologies on CD sales 'is statistically indistinguishable from zero' (Oberholzer & Strumpf 2005).

Probably I will never be able to determine the detailed impact of illegal file-sharing on the sales of recorded music. The consumer behaviour dynamics simply is too complex. However, it is vital to recognize that P2P file-sharing is an important Cloud-based music service, perhaps the most important one, and certainly the most widely used. As has already been mentioned, for every track legally purchased online, twenty tracks are downloaded from P2P networks (IFPI 2008). However, it is important not to make the same mistake as many record labels, when comparing these two ways of acquiring music. One track downloaded from a P2P network is not necessarily corresponding to one track purchased at a single-song-download service. Rather, the relation between P2P networks and single-song-download services (or CDs for that matter) should rather be compared to the relationship between libraries and bookstores. The consumer behaviour and rationale at P2P networks is quite different from a single-song-download retailer. At the single-song-download retailer, consumers are quite sure which songs they like or dislike before making the actual purchase. At P2P networks, consumers may download the entire Elvis Presley catalogue out of curiosity after having heard 'Jailhouse Rock'. They may choose to download songs which they have already purchased because they are using their laptop computer, and not the living room computer where those songs are stored. P2P file-sharing networks are Cloud-based music libraries rather than head-on competitors to single-song-download services. Do note that this does not imply that I argue that there is no impact from the use of online piracy on the legitimate music sales. The bulk of the reports presented during the last couple of years increasingly support the case that online piracy in aggregate has a negative effect on the sales of recorded music. This position has been held by most music firms from the very outset, and they have spent considerable resources trying to minimize the consumers' unsanctioned file-sharing activities and to bring back the control of music distribution from the hands of the audience.

Music firms' response to online piracy
Music firms, like most other rights holders, try to protect the value of their assets. The intellectual property portfolio often constitutes a major part of the music firm's balance sheet and if something or someone is threatening to diminish the value of the firm's assets it is the duty of the management to act. It is not the first time the music industry has been concerned about copyright infringement and the potential loss of distribution control. When the compact cassette technology was developed, it also incited a creative and social music listening culture with phenomena such as dubbing,[29] bootlegging[30] and mixtaping.[31] A whole range of new audience actions was opened up to the public. However, it was difficult to collect immediate revenues from the audience's new actions. The industry decided to respond by launching information campaigns such as IFPI's legendary 'Home taping is killing music – and it's illegal' initiative during the 1980s. The industry also successfully lobbied against governments in order to introduce a levy on cassette recorders and on blank, recordable cassettes. The levy would compensate copyright owners for the illegal use (e.g. dubbing) of the cassette technology. It should be noted that in some nations, for instance in the UK, the trade organizations did not want the blank cassette levy. They argued that, by introducing such a mechanism,

they were indirectly accepting copyright infringements, such as dubbing and bootlegging.

The response from the industry during this period has many parallels to how the industry responds to the impact from digital technologies. The strategic actions within this area have been documented by many scholars, for instance by Barfe (2004), Freedman (2003) and Imfeld (2004).

Several initiatives have been aimed directly at the consumers. First, information campaigns have been launched by various trade bodies. The purpose of these initiatives has been to influence the understanding and the attitudes, primarily among young people, about copyright-related issues. The international trade body of the recording industry, IFPI, is running the 'Pro Music' campaign in several music markets.[32] Its US affiliate RIAA has a similar initiative aimed for the domestic market called 'Music United',[33] and in the UK, music publishers operate the 'Respect the value of music' campaign, via the trade organization British Music Rights (BMR).

Second, an initiative primarily launched by trade organizations representing record labels consists of lawsuits filed against organizations and individuals who are violating copyright legislation. These lawsuits have been especially prevalent in the US market, where 18,000 cases have been filed by the RIAA during recent years. Trade organizations in Europe have been less aggressive and have only filed approximately 5500 lawsuits in eighteen countries (Millard 2006).

Third, the music recording industry has supported the development of various techniques to restrict and control the copying of music. However, these technologies have often failed, since some have made listening to CDs via certain players difficult, and others have seriously threatened the consumer's personal integrity (e.g. Borland 2005). In spite of all these and other similar initiatives intended to regain control and to stop illegal file-sharing, the P2P networks still elude the threats from the copyright industries. As the graph in figure 5.1 shows, in January 2006, there actually were more P2P network users than ever.

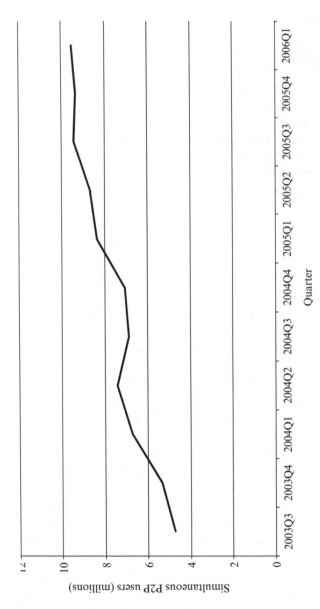

Note: The graph does not include BitTorrent users.

Source: BigChampagne

Figure 5.1. Continuing growth in numbers of simultaneous P2P users worldwide

Perhaps the single most enduring effect of these initiatives has been a negative impact on the reputation of the music industry. Entertainment industries, including the music industry, have long been suffering from a rather bad reputation. Negus recognizes this reputation by referring to music companies (in somewhat ironic terms) as 'commercial corrupters and manipulators' (Negus 1996:46). Other texts have used Hunter Thompson's provocative description of the television business to describe the music industry: 'Mainly I are dealing with a profoundly degenerate world, a living web of foulness, greed and treachery' (Thompson 1988:43).

Music industry decision-makers are well aware of the damage that their efforts to regain the distribution control cause to their already injured reputation. Nevertheless they see no other option but to do everything possible in order to sustain the value of their intellectual properties: 'it just looks like I are anti every new technology that comes around . . . but that's not true really, I mean sometimes it is true but that is for good reason, for good business reason. That's hard to get across to the media or the public . . .' (trade organization representative).

Another kind of strategic initiative that has proved more effective has been to lobby multilateral organizations and governments to revise copyright treaties and legislations. In 1996, the 183 member states of the World Intellectual Property Organisation (WIPO) adopted the WIPO Copyright Treaty. The aim was to adapt the copyright treaty to the development of digital information and communication technologies. The treaty ensured among other things that computer software was protected by the copyright legislation in the member states. This treaty has, since 1996, slowly been implemented: in the US as the Digital Millennium Copyright Act (DMCA) in 1998 and in the EU as the European Union Copyright Directive (EUCD) in 2001. Almost all the individual member states of the EU have since 2001 implemented the EUCD in their national legislations. In the countries where the treaty has been implemented, copyright legislation has generally been tightened and the punishment for infringing and violating the legislation has been increased.

It is not possible to attribute the revised copyright legislation among WIPO member states entirely to copyright industry lobbying. However, the tightening process that has been going on during the last decade has been eagerly applauded by the copyright firms. It is still too early to say what effect these legislations will have on the illegal file-sharing activities. At least so far, the P2P-based file-sharing activity continues to grow. However, the new legislations provide tools for rights holders to act more aggressively and maybe they will eventually use these tools to their full capability.

If that were to happen, music firms would probably be able to increase the level of control, decrease the network connectivity and increase their revenues from various audience actions. However, the level of control has an inverse relationship with the level of accessibility. The more tightly you control your content the more difficulty consumers will have in accessing and gaining awareness of that content. Following such a path would have a hampering effect on the audience–media engine, which in turn would work against or maybe even cancel out any revenue increase caused by the improved control.

The audience as amateur musicians

During the days of analogue media technologies, the ability to create high-quality media artefacts was restricted to those who had access to expensive facilities and tools for professional audio and video production. As I have discussed in previous chapters, digital technologies have dramatically changed this situation and made it possible for anyone equipped with an ordinary laptop to create and upload sounds and images of at least semi-professional quality.

This development, combined with the audience's improved access to digital sounds and images online, has opened up what often is referred to as a 'remix culture' (e.g. Tapscott & Williams

2006:137). Remix culture is closely related to Jenkins's participatory culture, but emphasizes the phenomenon of consumers' using bits and pieces of existing popular culture to create new meanings and new artefacts. This kind of cultural recycling is manifested in several ways in the area of music.

One example is what is known as 'plunderphonics', a term coined by John Oswald in 1985 to denote musical works solely made out of samples of existing recordings. Another instance of musical recycling is the 'mash-up', which is a musical work made by remixing instrumental sound from one song with the vocals from another. While the majority of user-generated plunderphonics and mash-ups are most likely to end up as an obscure blog-post, some (almost) professional artists have also picked up the technique and created works which actually reached a relatively respectable level of recognition. Prank Monkey's 'London booted' from 2004, primarily based on the Clash's 'London calling' from 1979, is one fine example, and Danger Mouse's *Grey Album* from the same year which combined The Beatles' *The White Album* (1968) with Jay-Z's *The Black Album* (2003) is another one. Jay-Z's *The Black Album* is also interesting for another reason, since that album includes a capella versions of the tracks, specifically to facilitate new remixes and mash-ups. Perhaps it is not entirely surprising that a hip-hop artist such as Jay-Z makes such a move, since musical recycling and sampling also is at the core of hip-hop culture. However, it shows how the concepts of remix culture have been picked up by the established producers.[34]

Another manifestation of remix culture is the creation of fan-videos based on a popular song. This phenomenon has gained strong momentum together with YouTube's positioning as the leading website for all kinds of user-generated videos. There are many different kinds of fan-videos: some are slideshows intended to illustrate a user's sincere interpretation of a song and others are home-made videos of a fan impersonating the artist, often with an ironic twist.

Some fan-videos are more technically sophisticated, being created by editing short clips into a coherent video. The conventions and aesthetics of the videos vary. One important genre is the Anime Music Video (AMV) which is made out of short clips from Japanese Anime movies where the characters' lip movements are synched with the lyrics of the song. As so often in the pop cultural sphere, conventions, values and fads are shaped through a conversation between a creative audience and the professional pop cultural creators. In the case of AMVs, the team behind Britney Spears chose to use Anime aesthetics when creating Spears's 2008 music video 'Break the Ice'. However, some of Spears's fans did not approve of the video, which did not follow the traditional Britney Spears video format. As a response, Philip Campbell Jr, a Britney fan from Snohomish in the US decided to make his own version of the 'Break the Ice' video, based on clips from Spears's older music videos and stage performances. In June 2008, the official video had more than 8 million views on YouTube, but Campbell's video actually received more than 2 million views, which is a fairly impressive number for a court reporter from Snohomish.

Another interesting genre is the Slash music video which normally tells a homoerotic story where characters from one narrative are given new meanings by combining the right sounds with the right images. For some reason it has become very popular to use the *Star Trek* characters Mr Spock and Captain Kirk as the basis for such Slash music videos. Fans have created numerous videos around these characters, based on songs such as Justin Timberlake's 'SexyBack', Nine Inch Nails's 'Closer' and Divinyls's 'I Touch Myself'. While irony is an important ingredient in many fan-videos, several videos are made with what at least seems to be complete sincerity and true appreciation of the artist. The fan-made 'Break the Ice' video mentioned above probably belongs to that category, together with many other fan-made videos of songs in almost every thinkable musical genre.

The amount of user-generated online content is growing at a staggering rate and the examples above are only a few samples taken from a wide range of works generated by creative fans. During the analogue age, there were many hurdles to be overcome before a writer, composer, artist or any human being for that matter could get their works known to the world. The very process of getting your work published was defining for many such professions; for instance you were a writer if you had a book accepted by a publisher. In the digital age, anyone can get published, and anyone can be a writer. There are of course still many hurdles before the work of an artist or writer will reach into the audience's awareness zone, but at least today both the distribution and the production bottlenecks are almost entirely gone. Every day, 175,000 new weblogs are launched, and 1.6 million new posts are published. YouTube, the largest web community for user-generated videos, claims that ten hours of video content is uploaded to their service every minute.

This development takes us towards an interesting future where the ratio between the amount of professionally generated content and the amount of user-generated content available online is asymptotically approaching zero. In other words, almost all content available online is user-generated and only a small fraction is created by those people who actually write texts, make movies or sing songs professionally. In a world coloured by the virtues of the remix culture it will become virtually impossible to charge users for simple access to content (cf. the discussion in chapter 3). It is interesting to speculate how such a development will affect the professional production of popular culture. Probably it will be increasingly difficult to create profitable entertainment projects such as full-length motion pictures or traditional music albums. In order to survive, the producers should rather focus on providing tools and building blocks for the users to create their own material. Surely, something which is similar to the traditional movie or album could also be provided, merely as an example of how the building blocks might be put together, but what is most important is to offer a service which inspires and stimulates the users' creativity (cf. the Nine Inch Nails case on p. 1). By creating such a service it would be possible to attract the users' attention for minutes or hours and to be able to charge advertisers for the immediate access to the users' open minds.

Music promotion goes viral

One of the themes running through this study of the new music economy is the music firms' loss of control. Above, I discussed the loss of *distribution* control, but music firms also have less control of other parts of the music business value chain. One such area is the promotion of music.

One significant trend which has changed the rules of music promotion is the growing importance of Internet-based social network services. An Internet-based social network service allows people who share a common interest of some kind to communicate, cooperate and socialize. The notion of connecting a set of computers in order to facilitate social networking is fundamentally linked with the early development of the Internet during the 1970s. Two pioneering services of very different character which still are in operation are Usenet, launched in 1979, and the Well, launched 1985. While these early social network services primarily were focused on discussion between people, the contemporary social networks support other kinds of communicative actions. Certainly, social network services such as Bebo, MySpace, Facebook, Lunarstorm, LinkedIn etc., allow users to discuss various topics, but more important than the discussion, are the users' *public presentation* of themselves. Users are able to present a character, real or fake, in a personal homepage within the service. Social network services are offered with different purposes and different target audiences, and, depending on the focus of the service, the users' homepage differs greatly. However, if I allow ourselves to focus on the social networks primarily aimed at the younger audience, the homepage is a life-style and identity marker as important as your clothes, your voice and your haircut. A homepage should normally contain relatively static information such as sex, age, location, occupation, religious and political views, favourite music, movies and books. It should also be updated with recent and relevant information such as a short phrase describing the feeling one has right now, pictures of the food one just ate or links to a cool music video seen on YouTube. Most social network services offer features which allow users to search and process the homepage information of other users. For instance, to find lost childhood friends, to compare music preferences to find your musical twins in the network or to look at your friends' recent photos.

It is obvious that the information users reveal on their homepages is a goldmine to marketers of any consumer product or service, including music. By processing the homepage information it is in theory possible to locate very accurately those users who are likely to be interested in a specific artist or musical genre. Again in theory, it is possible to establish a close relationship between the artist and its audience within such a social network, and very accurately and cost-efficiently promote concert tickets, new albums, merchandise, etc. The problem is that, while this might be possible in theory, the relationships within social networks are typically not between consumers and brands, but between trusted friends with relationships already established in real life. This does not imply that social network users are unsusceptible to information about new products or services, but that such information preferably should be delivered by friends within the network, and not by Nike, Nokia or Orange.

This means that information diffusion in social networks normally follows a P2P, word-of-mouth pattern rather than the top-down traditional thirty-second-spot pattern. In word-of-mouth promotion, information is distributed voluntarily by one individual to another. I shall not get into the psychology behind what motivates an individual to perform such an action, but merely conclude that some texts, sounds, images and videos are indeed able to evoke such an audience response. This phenomenon is not new to the music industry, but there are numerous examples from the old music economy of how artists through an uncontrolled word-of-mouth process have gained a foothold in a certain territory or market. One such example from the analogue age concerns the Swedish pop act Roxette. Roxette was completely unknown in the US until Dean Cushman, an American exchange student from Minneapolis, brought a copy of the Roxette album *Look Sharp!* home from Sweden for the 1988 holiday break. Cushman urged a local Minneapolis radio station, KDWB 101.3 FM, to play the album and, based on positive feedback from callers, the station's programme director copied the album and distributed it to other stations. Within weeks *Look Sharp* became popular throughout the region, and ultimately nationwide. On 8 April 1989, the single 'The Look' reached the number one position of *Billboard*'s Hot 100 and eventually Roxette turned out to be one of the most successful Swedish exports since the days of ABBA (see e.g. *Billboard* 1989; Thorselius 2003).

Through the growing importance of social networks, these kinds of uncontrolled processes are no longer merely random flukes, but are slowly becoming more or less the norm of music promotion in the digital age. In the new music economy, music firms are increasingly dependent on their fans to create a strong media presence and to promote their music. The clever music firm does not have to shout louder, by increasing its marketing budget, in order to compensate for the raised audience fragmentation – it can promote its artists by supporting fans' desire to express themselves through the music.

The rapid information diffusion processes which take place in a friction-free network are extremely difficult to predict and control. Such a system is extremely sensitive to minor changes in its initial conditions, and insignificant events (as in the Roxette story) can lead to radical shifts in the system's behaviour. Often these processes are referred to as 'viral' since there are many similarities to how an air-borne viral disease spreads across an area. It is not uncommon that non-commercial user-based content, such as YouTube videos, funny jokes and websites, suddenly go viral. One of the more extreme examples probably is the Swedish baby boy William who was videotaped by his father while laughing quite adorably. The father posted the video on YouTube for his own mother to see, but lo and behold, one year later, the 1 minute 40 seconds long video has been viewed more than 50 million times and is one of the most viewed videos on YouTube, ever.

WHEN THE PROMOTION BECOMES THE ART FORM – YEAR ZERO BY NINE INCH NAILS

The Los Angeles-based 'industrial rocker' Trent Reznor, a.k.a. Nine Inch Nails, has a very loyal fan base. Reznor's music is violent, dark and dystopian and seems to appeal to a demographic consisting of computer-literate Quake*-playing young men. In 2007, Reznor released a project titled *Year Zero*. From one perspective, *Year Zero* adheres to traditional music promotion logic. A sixteen-track album was released and supported by a series of promotion activities aimed at Reznor's core audience, the computer-literate young men. However, from another perspective, *Year Zero* should not be considered as merely an album, but as interactive multi-media art, where the album is only one component among many others.

Besides being a concept album, where Reznor paints a dystopian vision of a world to come, *Year Zero* is also a so-called alternate reality game (ARG) which takes place in the physical world as well as online. A narrative is told by releasing subtle clues and puzzles which the players are supposed to discover and solve together. The 3.5 million fans playing *Year Zero* found clues as hidden messages on Nine Inch Nails's tour T-shirts, on USB memory sticks someone had forgotten in the bathroom at a concert venue, as cryptic video clips on YouTube and so on.

It would be close to impossible to create a successful ARG without using the Internet as a platform for communication. To solve a puzzle, fans might have to look for clues on different continents and combine the brains of a computer science graduate and an expert on Sumerian language. The 'hive mind' made up by the Internet-connected Nine Inch Nails fans solved many of these clues relatively quickly and they were thereby able to propel the narrative to the next phase.

Year Zero was produced by 42 Entertainment, a company which to a large extent has driven the evolution of ARGs as multimedia experiences/promotional tools. For instance, 42 Entertainment has previously worked with ARGs related to the *A.I.* motion picture, the Halo 2 video-game and Microsoft's Windows Vista.

It is of course naïve to deny that one important purpose of an ARG is to increase the sales of a product or improve the recognition and values of a brand. However, the ARG also delivers entertainment value which makes it into a fascinating experience by itself. In the music industry in the digital age it is difficult to say if the concert is promoting the album or if it is the other way round. The same reasoning is transferable to the relationship between an ARG and an album: is it really the ARG which is promoting the album or is it perhaps the other way round?

Links and additional resources related to this case can be found on the website: http://www.musicinthecloud.net

Quake is a first-person-shooter videogame developed by id Software.

While this may happen once in a while quite unexpectedly as in the William case or the Roxette case, it is not a viable communication strategy for a profit-maximizing music firm. The question is whether and how music firms are able to mimic the success of the user-generated content with viral potential. Is it possible to create a piece of digital information with the same kind of appeal as the laughing baby boy but which also carries a commercial message which resonates with the chosen target audience? A number of branded viral marketing campaigns have actually been relatively successful, but those campaigns generally have not only been a simple video-clip released on the Internet but rather immersive multimedia productions intended to involve and activate the user in some way or another. An example of such a 'marketing campaign' was the alternate reality game launched by Nine Inch Nails and the advertising agency 42 Entertainment in 2007 (see case study).

As Trent Reznor explained: 'The term "marketing" sure is a frustrating one for me at the moment. What you are now starting to experience IS "year zero". It's not some kind of gimmick to get you to buy a record – it IS the art form' (Marchese 2007). In other words, the game and the album should be considered as two equally important parts of an immersive multimedia experience. I recognize the parallels between Reznor's statement and the discussion regarding 'option value blurring' phenomenon on p. 90 above, and conclude that, in the new music economy, the distinction between promotional material and the 'actual experience' is rapidly disappearing.

Audience-driven talent development

Perhaps the most important capability of a record label is to develop unpolished talents into professional entertainers and recognized brands. This capability is comprised of different components such as financial resources, coaching skills, musical craftsmanship and the ability to see the potential superstars among the plethora of mediocre wannabes. At its core, the components of the talent-development process remain the same in both the old and the new music economy. For instance, still the most important and common way to develop a talent is through extensive touring. It is on stage that young artists slowly but surely will develop a musical craftsmanship, learn how to interact with an audience and to appreciate the romantic ambience in a tour bus from 1982. However, the empowerment of the audience does make some dents in this area as well, for instance in the financing of new talent development. Record labels usually invest in recording projects in the hope that they eventually will get a positive return on their investment. The money is needed for the actual recording but also for promoting the album to raise the awareness and demand among prospective fans.

Cloud-based services, such as social network services, enable a completely different way to provide funding for music projects, or for any kind of project for that matter. The concept is known as 'peer investing' and is best explained through an example. SellaBand.com is a social network service explicitly focused on music and is a place for unsigned artists as well as music lovers to meet. The unsigned artists are able to upload their home-made demos for the music lovers to enjoy. Those music lovers who appreciate the work of an artist and want to hear more can make an investment in that artist. The investors buy what SellaBand.

com calls 'parts' for $10 a pop and as soon as 5000 parts have been sold, the artist is assigned a producer and is given the opportunity to record a full-length album. Besides getting a CD for every part the investor owns, SellaBand.com has created a set of mechanisms which is supposed to provide incentives for the investors to promote the artist to their friends and the rest of the world. Among other things, the investors are given a share of the revenues from the adverts which are displayed on the SellaBand website.

Another aspect of the talent-development process affected by the evolution of Internet-based social network services is the arenas and the methods for spotting new talents. In the really old days, the A&R agents spent their nights at shady clubs and minor venues in the hope of discovering a talent before the competition did. When the compact cassette, the CD-R and eventually the MP3 format made low-cost music storage and distribution available to unsigned artists, the A&R agents also could stay at their desks and listen to the loads of demos sent to their offices by hopeful musicians. These new technologies changed the decision-making process considerably, partly because the A&R agents increasingly based their talent-spotting decisions on a recording rather than on a live performance.

Social network services open up yet another arena for the A&R agents' talent-spotting activities. MySpace and other similar social network services allow unsigned artists (or creative consumers if you prefer) to shortcut the A&R agent and present their own music directly to the other members of the network. Data and basic statistics describing how other users respond to the artist's music and image are able to support the A&R agents' decision-making. Such real-time market research data reduces the risk of overlooking talents which the audience loves but which the A&R agents are unable to recognize as artists with high potentials.

The conflict between consumers and rights holders

From a strictly contractual perspective, the majority of the creative and social music fans' activities are in breach of the stated conditions for using the content in question. The rights holders define the 'Terms of Use' in order to inform the audience what they can and cannot do without the holders' explicit permission. Usually, 'all rights' are reserved for the rights holder (cf. p. 18), and the buyer of a music recording is not allowed to duplicate, lease or publicly perform or broadcast the song without the explicit permission to do so. Similarly, music fans that without explicit permission upload a remix to their social network homepages, redistribute the song via email or file-sharing networks or use the music to create new music videos breach their agreements with the music firm. From a strictly contractual perspective, the music firm has the right to receive compensation for that unauthorized use and the potential damage they might have sustained.

However, often things are not as straightforward as that. While a successful court case might put a stop to a specific contractual breach and perhaps bring in some cash in the short term, it might have serious negative implications for the firm's business in the longer term. I have already discussed the importance of audience actions in raising media presence and promoting an artist. By discouraging fans from remixing and uploading music, music firms are by definition limiting this contribution to its media presence, which in turn has a negative impact on sales.

Another related problem is the link between the ability to control the distribution of an intellectual property and the consumers' ability to access that property. I know from previous discussions in this chapter that it is important to balance control and access. If the control is loose, many consumers will be able to enjoy the recorded music but the music firm will have difficulties in generating any revenues from that use. On the other hand, if the control is strict, only a few consumers will have access to the songs and will be able to learn to like them. In other words, a policy which implies that *every* contractual breach should be brought to trial would lead to a business performance below the optimal. The big question then is when to sue and when not to sue. There are several examples where rights holders have refrained from suing. For instance, in the case of the Britney Spears fan-video discussed above, Philip Campbell Jr, the creator of the video, actually sent the piece to the record label, which to this date has not given its permission to the video but neither has it reacted negatively to the unauthorized use of their content. One might argue that since the fan-video was made without any commercial intentions and without trying to hurt the Britney brand, probably even the most narrow-minded record label would choose not to sue Mr Campbell. However, in general it is difficult to define any universal rules and routines for how a music firm should respond to copyright infringement.

I recognize that some of the music fans' activities are seriously hurting the music firms' businesses and probably deserve to be brought to trial by the rights holders. However, I also argue that social and creative music use is the normal way music fans use music in the new music economy. In other words, it is not the consumers who are out of line and should be brought back into the corral; it is the rights holders who need to rethink their terms of use. One viable way forward might be the licensing scheme suggested by the non-profit organization Creative Commons, founded by Lawrence Lessig in 2001. The general thinking behind Creative Commons licensing is to introduce some flexibility in the relationship between rights holders and consumers of culture. According to traditional copyright licences, 'all rights' are reserved to the rights holder. In contrast, if an intellectual property is licensed to a consumer by the use of a Creative Commons licence, it is possible to give the consumer 'some rights', for instance to redistribute an unaltered work for non-commercial purposes, while 'some rights' still can be reserved for the rights holder. Such a model would be considerably more in tune with the new music economy and would be better able to balance the needs of both rights holders and consumers of culture.

6

Future Sounds

In this book I have laid out some of the most fundamental dynamics of the contemporary music industry. Based on this examination, I will in this last chapter sketch the contours of how the music industry may evolve in the future. It should be noted that the music industry is obviously as chaotic and unpredictable as any other complex dynamic system, and most attempts to make forecasts quickly become fairly ridiculous and futile. However, I believe it is indeed possible to explore, with some lasting relevance and value, at least some dimensions of future music industry development. In the first chapter I laid out the basic features of the new music industry dynamics and concluded that it is characterized by high connectivity and little control; music provided as a service; and increased amateur creativity. I will now revisit these three features in an attempt to figure out what might be waiting around the corner.

Connectivity vs. control

The most important of the three features, actually underpinning the other two, is related to the tension between connectivity and control. I have argued that music firms have lost the ability to control how their music is distributed and used. However, as I mentioned in the previous chapter, the battle between connectivity and control is far from over, as there are strong forces trying to limit connectivity and to regain control. During the last couple of years, I have witnessed how new copyright legislations have resulted in extended terms of copyright protection, harsher punishment for copyright infringers, better tools for rights holders to gather information about the use of their intellectual property and so on.

These observations might lead you to believe that the current loss of control is only temporary. Rights holders will soon have regained full control of their intellectual properties and things will go back to normal. People will resume their old consumer habits and pay for the music they desire, and music companies will once again be able to invest in long-term talent development. However, there are two main reasons why this simply will not happen. First, a democratic and free society is based on the right to anonymity and the free flow of information, regardless of whether it is online or offline. The problem is that, online, it is difficult to control one kind of information and leave all other kinds alone. This means that any attempt to control online communication, regardless of good intentions, may have severe anti-democratic consequences, including the risk of creating a society where private communication is monitored and the free flow of information is impossible. Even though history shows us that democracy should not ever be taken for granted, I both hope and believe that this is a price which the societies I think of as democratic and free will be unwilling to pay.

The battle between connectivity and control has been going on for decades. Stewart Brand once famously explained:

> Information Wants To Be Free. Information also wants to be expensive. Information wants to be free because it has become so cheap to distribute, copy, and recombine – too cheap to meter. It wants to be expensive because it can be immeasurably valuable to the recipient. That tension will not go away. It leads to endless wrenching debate about price, copyright, 'intellectual property', the moral rightness of casual distribution, because each round of new devices makes the tension worse, not better. (Brand 1987:202)

Even though this tension will never go away, the second argument for why things will not go back to normal concerns the changing character of this 'wrenching debate'. For decades, this battle has mainly been between Law and Technology.

However, the 'Connectivity side', which previously has been poorly organized and largely represented by faceless information-technological innovations, has slowly become an ideological force to be reckoned with. I have seen how new licence structures such as Creative Commons have gained ground, and I have seen how the Pirate Party (an anti-copyright European single-issue party) has won a seat in the European parliament. But how did this change happen?

Manuel Castells's concept of the 'Internet Culture' may help to shed some light on the issue. The Internet was, and still is, shaped within a specific social environment with its specific cultural characteristics. Castells (2001) argues that those fundamental cultural values and beliefs that permeated the social environment in which the Internet was once invented still influence most online activities. The roots of the Internet can, to a great extent, be found in the academic and scientific world and, although the Internet outgrew its academic birthplace many years ago, 'the scholarly tradition of the shared pursuit of science, of reputation by academic excellence, of peer review, and of openness in all research findings' continue to colour the culture of the Internet (2001:40).

The sharing of ideas and innovations which is essential to the scientific community is a practice which is equally fundamental in other related communities, such as the 'hacker[35] community'. Hackers cherish freedom above everything else – the freedom to create, access, change and distribute knowledge and information. The whole concept of being a hacker is based on the ability to work on a freely available software in order to improve it in some way, and then to share it with one's peers in a common pursuit to create a more perfect technological solution. This 'gift practice' is not only motivated by generosity but also the source of prestige, reputation and social esteem among the members of the community. The more creative and interesting solutions you share, the more prestige and reputation you gain (ibid.).

It is interesting to note that these values and beliefs, which originally were confined to the field of open-source software programming, have spread into the world of music, movies, books and most other kinds of digitizable culture. Richard Stallman, one of the main characters in the hacker culture, has often debated the music business:

> We can make the computer network the musician's ally. Imagine a convenient way to send somebody a dollar anonymously through the Internet: some sort of digital cash. Imagine that every time you read a book or listen to a recording, it displays a box on the side of the screen, which says 'click here to send a dollar to the writer or to the band'. If you like the band or the book you will send that dollar sometimes. (Stallman 2002)

Influential opinion makers such as Stallman, currently the President of the Free Software Foundation, and Lawrence Lessig, founder of Creative Commons, have been able to legitimize the criticism of the current copyright regime and have paved the way for a balanced ideological debate about the role of copyright in democratic societies. The battle between connectivity and control is no longer merely a battle between Technology and Law, but a serious political debate between politicians and members of parliaments around the world.

The new attention given to the copyright debate, in combination with the potential severe societal implications of further tightening the copyright legislation, lead to the conclusion that the steady development of ever stronger copyright legislation that I have seen during the twentieth century is about to come to its end. I am an optimist and believe in the strength of our democratic institutions and that it will be more or less impossible to tighten the copyright legislation further. Rather, I anticipate that, during the next couple of decades, copyright legislations will slowly but surely become increasingly balanced and flexible to the benefit of holders, makers and users of musical rights.

Context and content

One question which is often raised by music industry professionals is whether the business can ever survive without a strong and tight copyright legislation. Will there be a consumer business for recorded music? As was argued in chapter 3, it seems unlikely that the sale of individual songs or albums to consumers will be able to keep its historical position as the music industry's most important source of revenue. It is important to note that the consumer's diminishing willingness to pay for individual songs is not immediately caused by online music piracy. An even stronger influencing factor may come from different kinds of legitimate 'non-music' online services. Most consumer-oriented online services are free to use. They are often funded through advertising or some other kind of indirect revenue source. It seems to be very difficult to communicate to consumers that, while some services can indeed be sustained by advertising revenues alone, others cannot. Most consumers do not care whether the costs of producing high-quality journalism, movies or music sometimes are considerably higher than the costs of operating a webmail service or a social network service. Influenced by the values and beliefs of the 'Internet Culture', many consumers expect that, online, information should always be free to access, change and share. These values constitute a colossal challenge for every manager and executive, regardless of the copyright industry, who tries to monetize their content online.

This may have dire consequences for many copyright firms since the revenues online will basically be considerably lower than the corresponding revenues in the offline world. It still remains unclear who will be willing to pay for high-quality journalism when the physical newspaper is gone. It is equally unclear how music companies will be able to finance long-term investments in talent development or complex and creative studio recordings without full control of the pricing and distribution of recorded music. Regardless of these apparently insurmountable problems, those consumer business models for recorded music that were discussed in chapter 3 will be unviable as long as rights holders insist on getting 'offline royalties' from online services. Advertising-based music services compete on the same ad market as every other online service, and the prices they are able to charge their advertisers are determined by the ad market and not by music rights holders. This means that there is a limit to the ad revenues the online music services are able to get, and there is equally a limit to the royalties they can pay to music companies without quickly going bankrupt. If rights holders do not accept this reality, they will end up with no consumer revenues instead of at least some consumer revenue.

At the time of writing, Spotify is the legitimate online music service of the day. Spotify uses a freemium model, which means that they have one advertising-funded 'free' version and one premium version with more features and without ads. Spotify has been able to attract millions of users to its free version, it has caught the advertisers' attention, and it delivers substantial revenues to music rights holders (Dagens industri 2009). There are numerous online music services trying to be the final solution to the problem of the music industry. However, Spotify may indeed be an important milestone in the music industry's development since it is one of the first online music providers that seems to have been able to negotiate agreements with rights holders which are both sustainable and fair for all parties. It should be noted that Spotify is still in its early days and only available in a handful of European countries. It remains to be seen whether it is able to sign similar agreements with rights holders in major music markets such as Germany, Japan and the US.

The reason for Spotify's success is not that it offers an extensive music catalogue or that it has fair and decent relationships with rights holders. The primary reason for its success is simply that the service's features and structure are superior to those of its competitors. Put in other words, Spotify's competitive advantage is Context rather than Content. In an environment where the basic musical content is available for free only 'two clicks away', it is quite difficult to compete with basic access to that same content. The music consumer's problem is not to access the content, it is how to navigate, manage and manipulate the music in the Cloud and on their digital devices. At the moment, most online music services, including Spotify, provide only rudimentary contextual services – e.g. they offer consumers music recommendations based on their usage history, or they have multiple-platform support which will give consumers access to synchronized songs and playlists whether they are on the move or at home. However, when looking into the future of online music services, it seems as if the most interesting developments will take place within the field of contextual services. For instance, imagine a music service which is constantly attuned to the user's release of pheromones! I would definitely pay a premium for such a service! Fantasies aside, during the coming decade, I hope and believe that a plethora of contextual music services (with fair and balanced rights holder agreements) will emerge, which will answer to the diverse musical needs most users are still unaware they actually have.

Creativity as consumption

One such musical need which users already have discovered is the desire to be an active participant in the music-making: either to independently make their own music and share it with others or to be part of their idols' and role models' creative processes. This book started out by presenting the case of Nine Inch Nails and how Trent Reznor provided tools and building blocks to his fans and encouraged them to play with the music and develop their own songs and remixes. Another artist who has developed a very close relationship with her fans is the London-based singer and songwriter Imogen Heap. During the production of Heap's latest album *Ellipse*, she regularly published a video-blog in which she discussed the development of her musical ideas. Eventually she published forty video episodes on YouTube during the two years the album was in production. In each episode she played pieces of her music, explained her thinking and asked for feedback. About 50,000 fans regularly followed the blog and commented on what they saw. Heap picked up these comments, entered into a conversation with her fans using different types of digital channels, such as Twitter and Facebook, and allowed the feedback to influence her creative process. I have pointed at several examples of how the distinction between promotion and distribution is blurred in the new music economy and I argue that Imogen Heap's Twittering, YouTubing, blogging and what-have-you are more than promotion for upcoming albums and concerts – these activities are all part of an immersive multi-platform Imogen Heap experience. It is the combination of all the different pieces that enables her to build such a strong relationship with her fans and stimulate the fans' demand for more twitters, more video-blogs, more concert tickets and more music.

Imogen Heap and Trent Reznor are two artists who have been able to respond to their fans' creative desires. They have turned the fans' creativity into their own consumer proposition and have thereby been able to build a business with low churn and high ARPU (average revenue per user), to borrow terms from telecom operator lingua. Creativity as a mode of consumption has become increasingly common in most copyright industries, not only the music industry. In the videogame industry, many franchises are entirely based on user-generated content, but also in more traditional industries, such as news media, user creativity has become an ingrained part of the value proposition. Today it is as common for online news media companies to provide tools for their readers to comment on news articles and to upload their own images as it is to have a header and a byline.

This development calls for artists, musicians, producers and songwriters alike to question their musical as well as their business identities. What is the value they deliver to their consumers and their fans? Is the value really the music or is it perhaps something else? In the music industry of tomorrow, most of the value might very well be located in the tools and the building blocks which allow fans to gossip about their shared interest, to play and remix the sounds and the songs, and so on. If that is the case, what then does it mean to be a creative artist in the music industry? Who are your competitors? Perhaps the fiercest competition does not come from other comparable artists or bands but rather from other platforms which are able to facilitate fans' creative expression and social interaction – platforms such as World of Warcraft, Bebo or Harry Potter. If that is the case, is it even relevant to talk about a music industry at all?

Final words

This book has been about the music industry – I have examined how the industry has developed into its current state and I have shared some thoughts about how it may develop in the future. I have argued that music companies will not be able to regain the control of their intellectual property and that online music services will compete with their contextual features, rather than with content exclusivity. I also suggested that music consumption based on user creativity means that the industry is entering a new competitive field where the competition no longer is restricted to other musical artists but includes all kinds of platforms facilitating fans' creative expression. These are all very significant changes which transform the logic and dynamics of the music industry. This transformation has, and will continue to have, far-reaching implications for the industry. It will force companies out of business, it will create yet unknown opportunities for inventive entrepreneurs and it will change the creatives' and audiences' relationships with the musics they love. But although the industry may change, it will not die. In spite of the turbulent times, the love for music will not fade, and great music will continue to give us goose bumps and euphoria. There will always be a demand to make and to listen to music, and as long as this demand persists, there will be opportunities for organizations to connect creatives with sponsors, aggregators and audiences. Even when they all have moved into the Cloud.

Notes

1 *Ghosts I–IV* reached the number 2 spot on Amazon's list of top sellers, 29 April, 2008.
2 It was in 1999 when Shawn Fanning, at the time a student at Northeastern University in Boston, Mass., developed the Napster software.
3 The components listed during the seminar were: Music Licensing, Co-Marketing, Branding with New Tools, Non-Traditional Retail Space, Digital Distribution, Internet-Specific Content, Fan–Artist Relationship Management, Quality Control, Content Management System Structures, Legal Structures, Live Performance, Incorporation of Attention Economy, Principles in Marketing Strategies.
4 Cf. Bill Gates's vision of 'friction-free distribution' and 'friction-free capitalism' (Gates 1995).
5 The book was actually written while Horkheimer and Adorno were living in Pacific Palisades, California, but the research institute remained formally located at Columbia University.
6 Hesmondhalgh does not use the term interactive media, but rather he uses a combination of the terms 'Internet industry', 'electronic publishing' and 'video and computer games'. I believe that the term 'Interactive media' or 'interactive leisure software', which is the term suggested by the British CITF, is incorporating the terms suggested by Hesmondhalgh.
7 This is why marketing mechanisms such as reviews and ratings play important roles in the media consumers' purchasing process. Reviews and ratings provide some guidance which allows the consumer to make an informed decision even when it is difficult or impossible to get full access to the product before the actual purchase.
8 According to one of the music industry's trade organizations (IFPI 2004b), 100,000 new albums were released in 2004, which equals more than 250 albums per day. If each album contains ten songs, and each song lasts for $3^1/_2$ minutes, more than 8500 minutes of new music are released every day. This means that the avid consumer has

to listen to at least six songs simultaneously, 24/7, to be able to keep up.

9   On p. 54, the concept of the preselection system is applied to the music industry.

10 For instance, three of the four largest music companies in the world are directly or indirectly listed on the most important stock exchange for media firms, the New York Stock Exchange (NYSE). Warner Music has been listed on NYSE since May 2005. Sony Music is owned by Sony and Universal Music is controlled by Vivendi; both Vivendi and Sony, are listed on NYSE. EMI Group was listed on the London Stock Exchange until mid-2007 when it was acquired by the private equity firm Terra Firma and thereby removed from public trading (http://www.emigroup.com; http://www.londonstockexchange.com; http://www.nyse.com; http://www.sonymusic.com; http://www.umusic.com; http://www.wmg.com).

11 An algorithmic task is a task where the road to the solution is straightforward and obvious. A heuristic task has no predefined road to its goal. A heuristic task most often does not have a predefined goal either, but can end in many ways. An example of an algorithmic task is 'Make some muffins!'; an example of a heuristic task is 'Cure cancer!'

12 A 'record label' is an organization that releases a certain form of music with a certain brand, such as Motown (soul/R&B), Blue Note (jazz) or Roc-A-Fella (hip-hop/rap). Major multinational music firms usually own and control several labels; EMI Music, for instance, controls more than fifty different labels across the world.

13 Industrial organization economics or IO economics is a field of economics that studies the strategic behaviour of firms, the structure of markets and their interactions.

14 An ongoing example is the dominating retailer of Internet-distributed music content, Apple's iTunes Music Store. iTunes uses a proprietary copy-protection technology called Fairplay which restricts consumers from playing the music they have acquired on iTunes on any portable music player other than the Apple iPod. Consumers, who have purchased a set of songs on iTunes, will have to continue using the iPod if they want to be able to continue listening to their music when they are on the move. If they decide to switch to another non-Apple portable music player, they have to purchase the same songs all over again – system lock-in in practice (http://www.itunes.com).

15 The preselection system framework is discussed on p. 22.

References

Adorno, T.W. (1941). On Popular Music. *Studies in Philosophy and Social Sciences*, 9 (1):17–48.

Adorno, T.W. (1972). *Introduction to the Sociology of Music.* New York: Seabury Press.

Albarran, A.B., & Chan-Olmsted, S.M. (1998). *Global Media Economics – Commercialization, Concentration and Integration of World Media Markets.* Ames, Ia.: Iowa State University Press.

Alderman, J. (2001). *Sonic Boom: Napster, MP3 and the New Pioneers of Music.* London: Fourth Estate.

Almqvist, K., & Dahl, C. (2003). *Upplevelseindustrin 2003, statistik och jämförelser.* Stockholm: Swedish Knowledge Foundation.

Amabile, T.M. (1996). *Creativity in Context.* Boulder, Colo.: Westview Press.

Amabile, T.M. (1998). How to Kill Creativity. *Harvard Business Review*, 76 (5) 77–87.

Anderson, C. (2004). The Long Tail. *Wired Magazine*, 12 (10):170–7.

Anderson, C. (2006). *The Long Tail – Why the Future of Business is Selling Less of More.* New York: Hyperion.

Angwin, Julia, McBride, Sarah, & Smith, Ethan (2006). Record Labels Turn Piracy Into a Marketing Opportunity. *Wall Street Journal*, 18 October 2006. Retrieved 19 September 2008 from <http://online.wsj.com/public/article_print/SB116113611429796022-_5EZVscJYWWFqv1AmPvXCiOjJms_20071018.html>.

Ansoff, H.I. (1965). *Corporate Strategy.* New York: McGraw-Hill.

Argyris, C., & Schön, D. (1978). *Organizational Learning: A Theory of Action Perspective.* Reading: Addison-Wesley.

Aris, Annet, & Bughin, Jacques (2005). *Managing Media Companies – Harnessing Creative Value.* Chichester: John Wiley & Sons.

Attali, J. (1985). *Noise: The Political Economy of Music.* Minneapolis: University of Minnesota Press.

Bain, J.S. (1959). *Industrial Organization.* New York: Wiley.

Barfe, L. (2004). *Where Have All the Good Times Gone? – The Rise and Fall of the Record Industry.* London: Atlantic.

Barney, J. (1991). Firm Resources and Sustained Competitive Advantage. *Journal of Management*, 17 (1): 99–120.

Barrett, C. (2007). Is There Gold at the End of *In Rainbows? Music Week*, 13 October 2007:12–13.

BBC News (2006). Police Hit Major BitTorrent Site. *BBC New Online*, 1 June 2006. Retrieved 2 June 2006, from <http://news.bbc.co.uk/2/hi/technology/5036268.stm>.

Billboard Magazine. 1948–2008.

Bjälesjö, J. (2005). 'Hi, my name is Hultsfred . . .' – om en organisations hantering av kulturell och ekonomisk förändring. *Etnologisk skriftserie*:1. Etnologiska institutionen, Lund University, Sweden.

Borland, J. (2005). Sony CD Protection Sparks Security Concerns. *CNet News.com*. 1 November 2005. Retrieved 11 April 2006, from <http://news.com.com/Sony+CD+protection+sparks+security+concerns/2100-7355_3-5926657.html>.

Boulding, K.E. (1968). *Beyond Economics*. Ann Arbor: University of Michigan Press.

Boulding, K.E. (1978). *Ecodynamics: A New Theory of Societal Evolution*. Beverly Hills, Calif.: Sage Publications.

Boulding, K.E. (1981). *Evolutionary Economics*. Beverly Hills, Calif.: Sage Publications.

Brand, S. (1987). *The Media Lab: Inventing the Future at MIT*. New York: Viking.

Brown, J.S., Collins, A. & Duguid, P. (1989). Situated Learning and the Culture of Learning. *Educational Researcher*, 18 (1):32–41.

Brown, J., & Duguid, P. (1991). Organizational Learning and Communities-of-Practice: Toward a Unified view of Working, Learning, and Innovation. *Organization Science*, 2 (1).

Brulin, G., & Nilsson, T. (1997). *Läran om arbetets ekonomi – Om utveckling av arbete och produktion*. Stockholm: Rabén Prisma.

Brunner, R., & Brewer, G. (1971). *Organized Complexity*. New York: The Free Press.

Brynjolfsson, E., Hu, Y., & Smith, M.D. (2003). Consumer Surplus in the Digital Economy: Estimating the Value of Increased Product Variety at Online Booksellers. *Management Science*, 49 (11):1580–96.

Bukowsky, R., & Connor, T. (2005). Famed Hit Factory to Close: The Sound of Silence at Studio. *New York Daily News*, 4 February 2005. Retrieved 28 September 2009 from <http://www.nydailynews.com/archives/news/2005/02/04/2005-02-,04_famed_hit_factory_to_close_t.html>.

Burnett, R. (1990). Concentration and Diversity in the International Phonogram Industry. Ph.D. dissertation, Department of Journalism and Mass Communication, University of Gothenburg, Sweden.

Burnett, R., & Weber, R.P. (1989). Concentration and Diversity in the Popular Music Industry 1948–1986. Paper presented at 84th Annual American Sociological Association Conference, San Francisco, 9–13 August 1989.

Byrne, D., & Yorke, T. (2007). David Byrne and Thom Yorke on the Real Value of Music. *Wired*, 16 (1).

Carr, N. (2008). *The Big Switch: Rewiring the World, from Edison to Google.* New York: Norton.

Castells, M. (1996). *The Information Age: Economy, Society and Culture, Vol. 1, The Rise of the Network Society.* Oxford: Blackwell Publishers.

Castells, M. (2001). *The Internet Galaxy.* Oxford: Oxford University Press.

Caves, R.E. (2000). *Creative Industries: Contracts Between Art and Commerce.* Cambridge, Mass.: Harvard University Press.

CBO (2004). *A CBO Paper – Copyright Issues in the Digital Media.* The Congress of the United States, Congressional Budget Office. August 2004.

Chan-Olmsted, S.M. (2006). Issues in Strategic Management. In A.B. Albarran, S.M. Chan-Olmsted & M.O. Wirth (eds.), *Handbook of Media Management and Economics.* Mahwah, N.J.: Lawrence Erlbaum.

Coase, R. (1937). The Nature of the Firm. *Economica,* N.S. 4:386–405.

Cohen, Wesley M., & Levinthal, Daniel A. (1990). Absorptive Capacity: A New Perspective on Learning and Innovation. *Administrative Sciences Quarterly,* 35:128–52.

Coleman, M. (2003). *Playback: From the Victrola to MP3, 100 Years of Music, Machines, and Money.* New York: Da Capo Press.

Crocker, S. (1969). *Host Software.* UCLA: Network Working Group. 7 April 1969. Retrieved 10 March 2006 from <http://www.ietf.org/rfc/rfc1.txt>.

Cunningham, M. (1999). *Good Vibrations: A History of Record Production* 2nd edn. London: Sanctuary Publishing.

Cunningham, S. (2005). Creative Enterprises. In J. Hartley (ed.), *Creative Industries.* Oxford: Blackwell Publishing.

Cyert, R.M., & March, J.G. (1992 [1963]). *A Behavioural Theory of the Firm.* Englewood Cliffs, N.J.: Prentice Hall.

Dagens industri (2009). Nytt hopp inom musikbranschen. *Dagens industri,* 8 August 2009. Retrieved 20 September 2009 from <http://di.se/Avdelningar/Artikel.aspx?ArticleID=2009\08\08\347737&sectionid=Ettan>.

D'Arcangelo, G. (2007). Active Listening: Social Identity in the New Economy. Speech given at the San Francisco Bay Area Chapter of ACM SigCHI meeting, 13 May 2007. Retrieved 16 September 2008 from <http://www.baychi.org/calendar/20070313>.

DCMS (1998). *Creative Industries Mapping Document*, Department for Culture, Media and Sport (DCMS), London. Retrieved 1 March 2006, from <http://www.culture.gov.uk/global/publications/archive_1998/Creative_Industries_Mapping_Document_1998.htm>.

Denis, Corey (2008). *New Music Economy: Defined?*. Posted on the Pho email list 13 May 2008.

Denisoff, R.S. (1975). *Solid Gold: The Popular Record Industry*. New Brunswick: Transaction Publishers.

Denisoff, R.S. (1988). *Inside MTV*. New Brunswick: Transaction Publishers.

Dowd, T.J. (2000). Music Diversity and the U.S. Mainstream Recording Market, 1955 to 1990. *Rassegna Italiana di Sociologia*, 41:223–63.

Dowd, T.J. (2002). Introduction: Explorations in the Sociology of Music. *Poetics*: 30:1–3.

Dowd, T.J. (2004). Concentration and Diversity Revisited: Production Logics and the U.S. Mainstream Recording Market, 1940–1990. *Social Forces*, 82 (4):1411–55.

Edison Media Research (2003). *The National Record Buyers Study*, 3. 23 June.

Eliot, M. (1990). *Rockonomics: The Money Behind the Music*. New York: Omnibus.

Elster, J. (1983). The Crisis in Economic Theory. *London Review of Books*, 4 (9):5-7. Retrieved 11 July 2006, from <http://www.geocities.com/hmelberg/elster/ar83ciet.htm>.

EMI (2002a). *EMI Annual Report 2002*. Retrieved 2 March 2006, from <http://www.emigroup.com/Financial/Default.htm>.

EMI (2002b). *EMI/Mariah Carey Part Ways*. EMI Corporate press release. 23 January 2002. Retrieved 26 February 2003 from <http://www.emigroup.com/Press/2002/press23.htm>.

EMI (2004). *EMI Announces Steps to Further Strengthen its Business*. EMI Corporate press release. 31 March 2004. Retrieved 7 April 2006, from <http://www.emigroup.com/Press/2004/press6.htm>.

EMI (2007). *EMI Annual Report 2007*. Retrieved 14 December 2007, from <http://www.emigroup.com/Financial>.

EMI (2008). *EMI Music and Papa Joe Records Announce Distribution Partnership*. EMI Corporate Press release. 12 May 2008. Retrieved 19 September 2008, from http://www.emigroup.com/Press/2008/press58.htm.

Enders Analysis (2003). *Piracy – Will it Kill the Music Industry?* March 2003.

England, R.W. (ed.). (1994) *Evolutionary Concepts in Contemporary Economics*. Ann Arbor: University of Michigan Press.

Engström, A., & Hallencreutz, D. (2003). *Från A-dur till bokslut – Hårda fakta om en mjuk industri*. IUC Musik & Upplevelseindustri. December 2003.

ExMS (2005). *The Export Performance of the Swedish Music Industry – An Update for the Year 2004*. Retrieved 2 June 2006, from <http://www.exms.se/export/export_performance_MI2005.pdf>.

Ferguson, D.A. (2006). *Industry-Specific Management Issues*. In A.B. Albarran, S.M. Chan-Olmsted & M.O. Wirth (eds.), *Handbook of Media Management and Economics*. Mahwah, N.J.: Lawrence Erlbaum.

Fisher, F. (1961). On the Cost of Approximate Specification in Simultaneous Equation Estimation. *Econometrica*, 29:139–70.

Florida, R. (2002). *The Rise of the Creative Class: And How It's Transforming Work, Leisure, Community and Everyday Life*. New York: Basic Books.

Forbes (2007). Top Earning Dead Celebrities. 20 July 2007.

Forrester Research (2003). *Downloading Music Hurts Europe's CD Sales*. January 2003.

Foster, J., & Metcalfe, J.S. (eds.) (2001). *Frontiers of Evolutionary Economics: Competition, Self-Organization and Innovation Policy*. Cheltenham: Edward Elgar.

Freedman, D. (2003). Managing Pirate Culture: Corporate Responses to Peer-to-Peer Networking. *The International Journal on Media Management*, 5 (3):173-9.

Frith, S. (1978). *The Sociology of Rock*. London: Constable.

Frith, S. (1983). *Sound Effects*. New York: Pantheon.

Frith, S., & Marshall, L. (eds.) (2004). *Music and Copyright* 2nd edn. Edinburgh: Edinburgh University Press.

Gates, B. (1995). *The Road Ahead*. New York: Penguin Books.

Gelatt, R. (1977). *The Fabulous Phonograph: 1877–1977*. New York: Collier.

Gerstner, L.V. (2002). *Who Says Elephants Can't Dance?: Leading a Great Enterprise Through Dramatic Change*. New York: HarperCollins.

Ghemawat, P. (1991). *Commitment: The Dynamics of Strategy*. New York: Free Press.

Gibbons, F. (2002). Robbie Williams Signs £80m Deal. *Guardian*, 3 October 2002. Retrieved 29 September 2008, from <http://www.guardian.co.uk/uk/2002/oct/03/arts.artsnews>.

Girard, A. (1981). A Commentary: Policy and the Arts – the Forgotten Cultural Industries. *Journal of Cultural Economics*, 5 (1):61–8.

Glassman, R.B. (1973). Persistence and Loose Coupling in Living Systems. *Behavioral Science*, 18:83–98.

Goodman, F. (2008). Rock's New Economy: Making Money When CDs Don't Sell. *Rolling Stone Magazine*, 29 May 2008. Retrieved 16 September

2008, from <http://www.rollingstone.com/news/story/20830491/ rocks_new_economy_making_money_when_cds_dont_sell>.

Graff, G. (2003). Rolling Stones Start Up The New Year With Ford. *Yahoo! Launch*. 6 January 2003. Retrieved 3 April 2006, from <http://launch. yahoo.com/read/story/12054919>.

Gronow, P. (1983). The Record Industry: The Growth of a Mass Medium. *Popular Music*, 3:53–77.

Gronow, P., & Saunio, I. (1998). *An International History of the Recording Industry*. London: Cassell.

Hadenius, S., & Weibull, L. (2003). *Massmedier (8:e upplagan)*. Stockholm: Albert Bonniers Förlag.

Hallencreutz, D. (2002). Populärmusik, kluster och industriell konkurrenskraft. Ph.D. dissertation, Department of Economic Geography, University of Uppsala, Sweden.

Hamel, G., & Prahalad, C.K. (1993). Strategy as Stretch and Leverage. *Harvard Business Review*, 71 (2):75–84.

Hamilton, D.B. (1953). *Newtonian Classicism and Darwinian Institutionalism: A Study of Change in Economic Theory*. Albuquerque: University of New Mexico Press.

Hansson, N. (2004). Kommentar: Tom Waits? Idol i TV4? Inte en chans!. *Dagens Nyheter*. 19 September 2004.

Hartley, J. (ed.) (2005). *Creative Industries*. Oxford: Blackwell Publishing.

Hartley, J. (2007). The Evolution of the Creative Industries – Creative Clusters, Creative Citizens and Social Network Markets. In *Proceedings Creative Industries Conference, Asia-Pacific Weeks*, Berlin.

Hax, A.C., & Wilde, D.L. (2001). The Delta Model: Discovering New Sources of Profitability in a Networked Economy. *European Management Journal*, (9) 4:379–91.

Hesmondhalgh, D. (2002). *The Cultural Industries*. London: Sage Publications.

Hirsch, P.M. (1970). *The Structure of the Popular Music Industry*. Survey Research Center, Ann Arbor: University of Michigan.

Hirsch, P.M. (1972). Processing Fads and Fashions: An Organisational Set Analysis of Cultural Industry Systems. *American Journal of Sociology*, 77:639–59.

Hirsch, P.M., & Fiss, P.C. (2000). Doing Sociology and Culture: Richard Peterson's Quest and Contribution. *Poetics*, 28:97–105.

Hollifield, C.A. (2003). The Economics of International Media. In A. Alexander, et al. (eds), *Media Economics: Theory and Practice* (85–106). Mahwah, N.J.: Lawrence Erlbaum.

Horkheimer, M., & Adorno, T. (1944). *Dialektik der Aufklärung*

– *Philosophische Fragmente*. Published in English (1972) as *Dialectic of Enlightenment*. New York: Seabury.

Horowitz, B. (2006). Creators, Synthesizers, and Consumers. *Elatable*, 17 February 2006. Retrieved 16 September 2008. from <http://www.elatable.com/blog/?b=5>.

Hoskins, C., & McFadyen, S. (2004). *Media Economics*. Thousand Oaks: Sage Publications.

Howkins, J. (2001). *The Creative Economy. How People make Money from Ideas*. London: Allen Lane.

IFPI (2004a). *The Online Music Report 2004*. The International Federation of the Phonographic Industry. London.

IFPI (2004b). *The Recording Industry in Numbers 2004*. The International Federation of the Phonographic Industry. London.

IFPI (2007). *The Recording Industry in Numbers 2007*. The International Federation of the Phonographic Industry. London.

IFPI (2008). *The Digital Music Report 2008*. The International Federation of the Phonographic Industry. January 2008. London.

IFPI (2009). *Recorded Music Sales 2008*. The International Federation of the Phonographic Industry, London. Retrieved 13 November 2009 from <http://www.ifpi.org/content/library/Recorded-Music-Sales-2008.pdf>.

Imfeld, C.J. (2004). Repeated Resistance to New Technologies: A Case Study of the Recording Industry's Tactics to Protect Copyrighted Works in Cyberspace between 1993 and 2003. Ph.D. dissertation, University of North Carolina at Chapel Hill.

Ipsos-Reid (2002). *Digital Music Behavior Continues to Evolve*. February 2002.

Jenkins, H. (2006). *Convergence Culture – Where Old and New Media Collide*. New York: New York University Press.

Joyce, M. (1987). *Afternoon, A Story* [CD]. Watertown, Mass.: Eastgate Systems.

Kaldor, N. (1972). The Irrelevance of Equilibrium Economics. *The Economic Journal*, 82:1237–55.

Kapferer, J.-N. (2004). *The New Strategic Brand Management – Creating and Sustaining Brand Equity Long Term* 3rd edn., London: Kogan Page.

Karlsson, D., & Lekvall, L. (2002). *Den ofrivillige företagaren*. Nätverkstan Kultur i Väst. Mars 2002.

Katz, M. (2004). *Capturing Sound – How Technology has Changed Music*. Berkeley: University of California Press.

Kealy, Edward (1982). Conventions and the Production of the Popular Music Aesthetic, *Journal of Popular Culture*, 16:100–15.

Keller, M. (2006). Sweden Pulls the Plug on Pirate Bay. *Los Angeles Times*, 1 June 2006. Retrieved 2 June 2006, from <http://www.latimes.com/business/la-fi-piratebay1jun01,1,545844.story>.

Knight, J.A. (1998). *Value-Based Management*. New York: McGraw-Hill.

Korte, E. (2005). Panel discussion: Music for Images. [Korte was at the time VP Music Director at Saatchi & Saatchi, New York.] Midem Conference, Cannes, France. 25 January 2005.

Kusek, D., & Leonard, G. (2005). *The Future of Music: Manifesto for the Digital Music Revolution*. Boston, Mass.: Berklee Press Publications.

Lave, J., & Wenger, E. (1991). *Situated Learning: Legitimate Peripheral Participation*. Cambridge: Cambridge University Press.

Levine, R., & Werde, B. (2003). Superproducers – They're Reinventing the Sound of Music, and the Music Industry. *Wired Magazine*, 11 (10):124–37.

Leyshon, A. (2001). Time-Space (and Digital) Compression: Software Formats, Musical Networks, and the Reorganisation of the Music Industry. *Environment & Planning A*, 33:49–77.

Liebowitz, S. (2002a). Record Sales, MP3 Downloads, and the Annihilation Hypothesis. Working Paper, School of Management, University of Texas, Dallas. 22 August 2002.

Liebowitz, S. (2002b). *Re-thinking the Network Economy*. New York: Amacom.

Lister, M., Dovey, J., Giddings, S., Grant, I., & Kelly, K. (2003). *New Media: A Critical Introduction*. London: Routledge.

Lorenz, H.-W. (1989). *Nonlinear Dynamical Economics and Chaotic Motion*. Berlin: Springer-Verlag.

Lowry, T. (2008). Look Who's Doing O.K. in the Music Business. *Business Week*, 4110 (90).

MacQueen, H., Waelde, C., & Laurie G. (2007). *Contemporary Intellectual Property – Law and Policy*. Oxford: Oxford University Press.

Madonna.com (2008). Robyn to Support Madonna's 'Sticky & Sweet' Tour. Press release. 17 June 2008. Retrieved 18 September 2008, from <http://www.madonna.com/news/index.php?mode=list&page=3>.

March, J.G., & Olsen, J.P. (1976). *Ambiguity and Choice in Organizations*. Bergen: Universitetsforlaget.

March, J.G., & Simon, H.A. (1958). *Organizations*. New York: Wiley.

Marchese, D. (2007). Further Down the Spiral. *The Salon*, 16 March 2007. Retrieved 19 March 2009, from http://www.salon.com/ent/audiofile/2007.03/16/nine_inch_nails>.

Mermigas, D. (2006). Cable Must Draw Guns for New-Media Battles. *The Hollywood Reporter*. 18 April 2006. Retrieved 18 April 2006, from <http://www.hollywoodreporter.com/thr/columns/mermigas.jsp>.

Meyer, J. and Rowan, B. (1978). The Structure of Educational Organizations. In M. Meyer (ed.), *Environments and Organizations*. San Francisco: Jossey Bass.

Miège, B. (1979). The Cultural Commodity. *Media, Culture and Society*, 1:297–311.

Miles, R.E., & Snow, C.C. (1978). *Organizational Strategy, Structure and Process*. New York: McGraw-Hill.

Miles, R.E., Snow, C.C., Meyer, A.D., & Coleman, H.J. (1978). Organizational Strategy, Structure and Process. *Academy of Management Review*, July:546–62.

Millard, E. (2006). Music Industry Files 2,000 More Lawsuits. *Newsfactor Magazine Online* 4 April 2006. Retrieved 5 April 2006, from http://www.newsfactor.com/story.xhtml?story_id=01000000094IY.

Mitchell, G. (2005). Prince of a Deal. *Billboard Magazine*, 117 (52):20.

Moorefield, V. (2005). *The Producer as Composer: Shaping the Sounds*. Cambridge, Mass.: The MIT Press.

Myrdal, G. (1956). *Development and Under-Development: A Note on the Mechanism of National and International Economic Inequality*. Cairo: National Bank of Egypt.

Negus, K. (1992). *Producing Pop – Culture and Conflict in the Popular Music Industry*. London: Arnold.

Negus, K. (1996). *Popular Music Theory*. Cambridge: Polity Press.

Negus, K. (1997). The Production of Culture. In P. du Gay, (ed.). *Production of Culture/Cultures of Production*. London: Sage Publications.

Negus, K. (1999). *Music Genres and Corporate Cultures*. London: Routledge.

Negus, K., & Pickering, M. (2004). *Creativity, Communication and Cultural Value*. London: Sage Publications.

Nelson, R., & Winter, S. (1982). *An Evolutionary Theory of Economic Change*. Cambridge, Mass.: Harvard University Press.

Neuman, W.R. (1991). *The Future of the Mass Audience*. Cambridge: Cambridge University Press.

New York Times (2008). In Rapper's Deal, a New Model for Music Business. 3 April 2008.

Oberholzer, F., & Strumpf, K. (2005). The Effect of File Sharing on Record Sales: An Empirical Analysis. Working Paper, Harvard Business School & University of North Carolina at Chapel Hill. June 2005.

O'Connor, J. (2000). *Cultural Production Strategy*. Information for Cultural Industries Support Services, Manchester. Retrieved 5 January 2006, from <http://www.mmu.ac.uk/h-ss/mipc/iciss/home2.htm>.

OECD (2005a). *OECD Broadband Statistics*. June 2005. Retrieved 2 March 2006 from http://www.oecd.org/document/16/0,2340,en_2825_4956 56_35526608_1_1_1_1,00.html.

OECD (2005b). *Working Party on the Information Economy, Digital Broadband Content: Music.* Organisation for Economic Co-operation and Development, Directorate for Science, Technology and Industry, Committee for Information, Computer and Communications Policy. 8 June 2005. DSTI/ICCP/IE(2004)12/Final.

Olin-Scheller, C., & Wikström, P. (2009). *Fan-fiction in a Scandinavian Context* (forthcoming).

Oram, A. (ed.) (2001). *Peer-to-Peer: Harnessing the Power of Disruptive Technologies.* Sebastopol: O'Reilly Media.

Orwall, B. (1995). Purple Drain. *Saint Paul Pioneer Press*, 15 January 1995.

Ouchi, W. (1978). Coupled versus Uncoupled Control in Organizational Hierachies. In M. Meyer (ed.), *Environments and Organizations.* San Francisco: Jossey Bass.

Pagrotsky, L. (2003). Upplevelseindustrin, i bred bemärkelse. Ministry of Industry. *Newsletter GURU.* 8 December 2003. Retrieved 13 January 2006, from <http://www.regeringen.se/sb/d/1352/a/4560>.

Parrack, D. (2008). Rolling Stones Leave EMI for Universal – Follow Radiohead, McCartney out the Door. *Brit Music Scene*, 26 July 2008. Retrieved 21 September 2009, from <http://www.britmusicscene.com/rolling-stones-leave-emi-for-universal-follow-radiohead-mccartney-out-the-door/>.

Perrow, Charles (1986). *Complex Organizations.* New York: Random House.

Peterson, R.A. (1976). *The Production of Culture.* Beverly Hills, Calif.: Sage Publications.

Peterson, R.A. (1979). Revitalizing the Culture Concept. *Annual Review of Sociology*, 5:137–66.

Peterson, R.A. (1982). Five Constraints on the Production of Culture: Law, Technology, Market, Organizational Structure and Occupational Careers. *Journal of Popular Culture*, 16:143–53.

Peterson, R.A. (1985). Six Constraints on the Production of Literary Works. *Poetics*, 14:45–67.

Peterson, R.A. (1994). Culture Studies through the Production Perspective, in D. Crane, (ed.) *The Sociology of Culture: Emerging Theoretical Perspectives.* Cambridge, Mass.: Blackwell.

Peterson, R.A. (2000). Two Ways Culture is Produced. *Poetics*, 28:225–33.

Peterson, R.A., & Berger, D. (1971). Entrepreneurship in Organizations: Evidence from the Popular Music Industry. *Administrative Science Quarterly*, 16:97–107.

Peterson, R.A., & Berger, D. (1975). Cycles in Symbol Production: The Case of Popular Music. *American Sociological Review*, 40:158–73.

Picard, R.G. (2002). *The Economics and Financing of Media Companies.* New York: Fordham University Press.

Picard, R. G. (2005). Unique Characteristics and Business Dynamics of Media Products. *Journal of Media Business Studies*, 2 (2):51–9.

Picard, R.G. (ed.) (2005). *Media Product Portfolios – Issues in Management of Multiple Products and Services*. Mahwah, N.J.: Lawrence Erlbaum.

Picard, R., & Wikström, P. (2008). Determinants of Domestic Music: An Empirical Analysis. Presented at the 8th World Media Economics and Management Conference, Lisbon, Portugal.

Pine, B.J., & Gilmore, J.H. (1998). Welcome to the Experience Economy. *Harvard Business Review* (July–August):97–105.

Poe, R. (1997). *Music Publishing: A Songwriter's Guide* 2nd edn, Cincinnati: Writer's Digest Books.

Porter, M.E. (1980). *Competitive Strategy: Techniques for Analyzing Industries and Competitors*. New York: Free Press.

Porter, M.E. (1990). *The Competitive Advantage of Nations*. London: Macmillan.

Porter, M.E. (1991). Towards a Dynamic Theory of Strategy. *Strategic Management Journal*, 12:95–117.

Power, D. (2002). 'Cultural Industries' in Sweden: An Assessment of their Place in the Swedish Economy. *Economic Geography*, 78 (2):103–28.

Power, D. (ed.) (2003). *Behind the Music – Profiting from Sound: A Systems Approach to the Dynamics of the Nordic Music Industry*. Nordic Council of Ministers, Nordic Industrial Fund, Center for Innovation and Commercial development.

Qualen, J. (1985). *The Music Industry: The End of Vinyl*. London: Comedia.

Radzicki, M.J. (1990). Institutional Dynamics, Deterministic Chaos, and Self-Organizing Systems. *Journal of Economic Issues*, 24 (1):57–102.

Radzicki, M.J., & Sterman, J.D. (1994). Evolutionary Economics and System Dynamics. In R.W. England (ed.), *Evolutionary Concepts in Contemporary Economics*. Ann Arbor: University of Michigan Press.

Rafaeli, S., and Sudweeks, F. (1994). *Project H Overview: A Quantitative Study of Computer-Mediated Communication*. Technical Report, University of Minnesota. ftp://ftp.arch.su.edu.au/pub/projectH/papers/techreport.txt.

Read, O., & Welch, W.L. (1976). *From Tin Foil to Stereo: Evolution of the Phonograph*. Indianapolis: Bobbs-Merrill and Howard W. Sams.

Reca, A.A. (2006). Issues in Media Product Management. In A.B. Albarran, S.M. Chan-Olmsted & M.O. Wirth (eds.), *Handbook of Media Management and Economics*. Mahwah: Lawrence Erlbaum.

Reuters (2006). Swedish Police Shut Web Site in Music Piracy Raid. *Reuters*, 31 May 2006. Retrieved 1 June 2006, from <http://news.com.com/Swedish+police+shut+Web+site+in+music+piracy+raid/2010-1030_3-6078588.html>.

Robinson, M. (2000). *The 'Sunday Times' 100 Greatest TV Ads*. London: Times Educational Services.

Rosen, C. (1994). Paisley Park, Warner Bros. Terminate Joint Venture. *Billboard Magazine*, 106 (7):5–6.

Schnur, S. (2005). Panel discussion: Music for Images. [Schnur was at the time World Wide Executive of Music at Electronic Arts.] Midem Conference, Cannes, France, 25 January 2005.

Schumpeter, J. (1911). *Theorie der wirtschaftlichen Entwicklung*. Published in English (1934) as *The Theory of Economic Development: An Inquiry into Profits, Capital, Credit, Interest, and the Business Cycle*. Cambridge, Mass.: Harvard University Press.

Schumpeter, J. (1942). *Capitalism, Socialism and Democracy*. New York: Harper.

Scott, A.J. (1999). The Cultural Economy: Geography and the Creative Field. *Media, Culture and Society*, 21:807–17.

Senge, P. (1990). *The Fifth Discipline*. London: Century Press.

Shapiro, C., & Varian, H.R. (1999). *Information Rules*. Boston, Mass.: Harvard Business School Press.

Simon, H.A. (1971). Designing Organizations for an Information-rich World. In M. Greenberg, (ed.), *Computers, Communications and the Public Interest*. Baltimore: Johns Hopkins University Press.

Simon, H.A. (1979). *Rational Decision-Making in Business Organizations*. Stockholm: The Nobel Foundation.

Simon, H.A. (1981). *The Sciences of the Artificial*. Cambridge, Mass.: MIT Press.

Simon, H.A., & Ando, A. (1961). Aggregation of Variables in Dynamic Systems. *Econometrica*, 29:111–38.

Smith, E. (2007). Madonna Heads for Virgin Territory; Concert Promoter Lures Material Girl From Warner Music With $120 Million. *Wall Street Journal*, 11 October 2007.

Stalk, G. (1988). Time – The Next Source of Competitive Advantage. *Harvard Business Review*, 66 (4):41–51.

Stalk, G., Evans, P., & Shulman, L. (1992). Competing on Capabilities. *Harvard Business Review*, 70 (2):57–69.

Stallman, R. (2002). Let's Share!. *www.openDemocracy.net* 30 May 2002. Retrieved 25 February 2003, from <www.openDemocracy.net>.

Sterman, J.D. (1989). Modeling Managerial Behavior: Misperceptions of Feedback in a Dynamic Decision Making Experiment. *Management Science*, 35 (3):321–39.

Sterman, J.D. (1994). Learning in and about Complex Systems. *System Dynamics Review*, 10:291–330.

STIM (2007). *STIM Annual Report 2006*. Retrieved 14 December 2007, from <http://www.stim.se>.

Stock, M. (2004). *The Hit Factory: The Stock, Aitken and Waterman Story*. London: New Holland Publishers.

Svenska Dagbladet (2004). Såpor skapar inte stjärnor. *Svenska Dagbladet*. 7 September 2004.

Tapscott, D. & Williams, A. (2006). *Wikinomics: How Mass Collaboration Changes Everything*. New York: Penguin.

Teece, D.J., Pisano, G., & Shuen, A. (1997). Dynamic Capabilities and Strategic Management. *Strategic Management Journal*, 18 (7):509–33.

The Irish Times (2006). Pussy Power? *The Irish Times – The Ticket*. 23 June 2006. Retrieved 17 October 2006, from <http://www.ireland.com/theticket/articles/2006/0623/>.

Thompson, H.S. (1988). *Generation of Swine: Tales of Shame and Degradation in the '80s*. New York: Simon & Schuster.

Thorburn, D., & Jenkins, H. (eds.) (2003). *Rethinking Media Change: The Aesthetics of Transition*. Cambridge, Mass.: The MIT Press.

Thorselius, R. (2003). *The Look for Roxette*. Stockholm: Premium Förlag.

Throsby, D. (2001). *Economics and Culture*. Cambridge: Cambridge University Press.

Towse, R. (2001). *Creativity, Incentive and Reward: An Economic Analysis of Copyright and Culture in the Information Age*. Cheltenham: Edward Elgar.

Towse, R. (ed.) (2002). *Copyright in the Cultural Industries*. Cheltenham: Edward Elgar.

Toynbee, J. (2000). *Making Popular Music – Musicians, Creativity and Institutions*. London: Arnold.

Tremlett, G. (1990). *Rock Gold: The Music Millionaires*. London: Unwin Hyman.

Varian, H. (1979). Catastrophe Theory and the Business Cycle. *Economic Inquiry*, 17:14–28.

Variety (1983). MTV Overtaking Radio as Motivation of Disc Purchases. *Variety*. 16 February:113.

Variety (1988). MCA Acquires Motown. *Variety*. November 24:32.

Vivendi (2007). Vivendi Annual Report 2006. Retrieved 14 December 2007, from <http://www.vivendi.com/ir/en/files/20070522_2006_annual_report.php>.

Vogel, H.L. (2001). *Entertainment Industry Economics*, 5th edn, Cambridge: Cambridge University Press.

von Bertalanffy, L. (1945). Zu einer allgemeinen Systemlehre. *Deutsche Zeitschrift für Philosophie*, 18 (3/4). Published in English (1950) as An Outline of General System Theory. *British Journal for the Philosophy of Science*, 1 (2):134–65.

von Neumann, J., & Morgenstern, O. (1944). *Theory of Games and Economic Behavior*. Princeton, N.J.: Princeton University Press.

Wallis, R. (1995). The Future of Radio as Seen from the Outside. *Nordicom-Information*, 1995 (1):11–23.

Wallis, R. (2004). Copyright and the Composer. In S. Frith, & L. Marshall, (eds.), *Music and Copyright* 2nd edn, Edinburgh: Edinburgh University Press.

Warner Music (2007). *Warner Music Annual Report 2006*. Retrieved 14 December 2007, from <http://investors.wmg.com/phoenix.zhtml?c=182480&p=irol-reportsannual>.

Watts, D.J. (2003). *Six Degrees: The Science of a Connected Age*. New York: Norton.

Weber, M. (1921). Die rationalen und soziologischen Grundlagen der Musik. Published in English (1958) as *The Rational and Social Foundations of Music*. Carbondale, Ill.: Southern Illinois University Press.

Weick, K. (1976). Educational Organizations as Loosely Coupled Systems. *Administrative Science Quarterly*, 21:1–19.

Wenger, E. (2006). *Communities of Practice – A Brief Introduction*. June 2006. Retrieved 21 September 2009, from <http://www.ewenger.com/theory/communities_of_practice_intro.htm>.

Werger, E. (1999) *Communities of Practice: Learning, Meaning, and Identity*. Cambridge: Cambridge University Press.

Wernerfelt, B. (1984). A Resource-based View of the Firm. *Strategic Management Journal*, 5 (2):171–80.

Wikström, P. (2005). The Enemy of Music – Modelling the Behaviour of a Cultural Industry in Crisis. *The International Journal on Media Management*, 7 (1 & 2):65–74.

Wikström, P. (2006). Reluctantly Virtual – Modelling Copyright Industry Dynamics. Doctoral dissertation, Media and Communication Studies, Karlstad University, Sweden.

Wikström, P. (2009). The Adaptive Behaviour of Music Firms – Introducing the Music Industry Feedback Model. *Journal of Media Business Studies*, 6(2): 67–96.

Wikström, P., & Burnett, R. (2009). Same Music, Different Wrappings. *Popular Music and Society*, 32 (4): 507–22.

Wildman, S.S. (2006). Paradigms and Analytical Frameworks in Modern Economics and Media Economics. In A.B. Albarran, S.M. Chan-Olmsted & M.O. Wirth (eds.), *Handbook of Media Management and Economics*. Mahwah, N.J.: Lawrence Erlbaum.

Witt, U. (2003). *The Evolving Economy – Essays on the Evolutionary Approach to Economics*. Aldershot: Edward Elgar.

Wolf, M.J. (1999). *The Entertainment Economy*. London: Penguin Books.

Yeaman, N. (2008). En kvinnlig Ziggy Stardust. *Dagens Nyheter*, 22 August 2008.

Zaid, G. (2003). *So Many Books: Reading and Publishing in an Age of Abundance*. Philadelphia: Paul Dry Books.

Index

360 degree model 139
42 Entertainment 163

A&R 54–5, 58, 100, 119–20,
   128–30, 142, 151, 166
ABBA 80, 126, 162
Absolute Music 133–4
Adams, Bryan 73
Adorno, T.W. 12–3, 28–9, 41
advertising 14, 17, 47, 56, 92, 95,
   97, 107–8, 126, 164, 174–5
AEG Live 60, 83
Albarran, A. B. 27
Alderman, J. 149
Almqvist, K. 15, 47
Amabile, T. M. 28–9
amateur 7–10, 85, 118, 134, 147,
   156, 170
Amazon 2, 103–4
Anderson, C. 90
Ando, A. 51
Angwin, J. 92
Ansoff, H.I . 34
Apple 66, 95, 101–4, 108, 112, 132
   Fairplay 102
   iPod 8, 66, 95, 102, 112
   iTunes 8, 66, 101–4, 108, 112
   Jobs, S. 101
Arctic Monkeys 80
Argyris, C. 36–7
Aris, A. 70
art and commerce 25, 29–30

Asylum 77
Attali, J. 49
audience fragmentation 10, 88–9,
   91, 95, 162
authenticity 25, 27–9

Backstreet Boys 121
Bain, J. S. 34
Barfe, L. 61–2, 153
Barney, J. 35
Beatles, The 80, 82, 119–20, 126,
   132, 157
Bebo 87, 160, 178
Berger, D. 41–3
Berliner, Emile 66, 73, 76
Berne Convention, the 18–19
Bertelsmann 73, 75
Billboard Magazine 66, 109, 131,
   144, 162
BitTorrent 8, 33, 154
Bjälesjö, J. 15
Black Eyed Peas 95
blogs 2, 87, 92, 147, 157, 159, 176
BMG 75–6, 82, 144
BMI 94
BMR 153
Bon Jovi 73, 121
Borland, J. 153
Boulding, K. E. 37
Bowie, David 80, 126
branding 1, 96, 118, 130, 133–6,
   140–1, 146, 164, 168

British Music Rights 153
Brown, J. S. 39, 41, 132
Brulin, G. 25
Brunner, R. 51
Brynjolfsson, E. 90
buckshot theory 24
Bughin, J. 70
business models 10, 53, 64, 85,
    93, 97–8, 101–2, 106, 108,
    115, 174
  ad-based 107–8
  all-you-can-eat 66, 104–5,
    114–15
  revenue-sharing 104–5, 108
  single-song download 103, 107,
    110, 113–14, 151

Capitol Records 63, 80–1
Carey, Mariah 73, 128
Carlsson, Andreas 121
Carlsson, Robyn 144–5
Carr, N. 4
Castells, M. 27, 43, 172
Caves, R. E. 16, 20, 23
CBS 63, 75–6
Chan-Olmsted, S. M. 20, 27
Cheiron Studios 121, 144
Chrysalis 81
CKX Entertainment 132
Clarkson, Kelly 135
Clear Channel 60, 83, 138
Coase, R. 26
Coca-Cola 92
Cohen, W. M. 36, 82
Columbia Records 12, 62, 66,
    75–6, 81
Compact Cassette 66
compilation 133
connectivity and control 5, 88,
    171, 173
copyright
  concepts 18

industries 9, 12–45, 53, 116,
    125, 153, 156, 177
  legislation 11, 17–18, 20, 43, 64,
    153, 155–6, 170, 173–4
Corey, D. 4
covermounts 112, 138
Creative Commons 168, 172–3
creativity 8–10, 14, 16, 25, 27–31,
    49–50, 85, 118, 122, 124, 159,
    170, 177–8
Crocker, S. 149
cultural industries 12–14, 16–7,
    41, 125
cultural production 30, 43
Cunningham, S. 14, 119, 123
Cyert, R. M. 27, 37

Dahl, C. 15, 47
Danger Mouse 157
DCMS 47, 48
Decca 63, 73–4
Def Jam Records 139
Denisoff, R. S. 24, 126
Denniz Pop 121, 144
Digital Millennium Copyright
    Act 155
Dion, Céline 7, 121
DMCA 20, 155
Dovey, J. 89
Dowd, T. J. 41, 145
Dr Dre 77
Duguid, P. 39, 41
Dylan, Bob 75, 82, 126
dynamic capabilities 36

Edge Group, The 139
Edison, T. A. 62, 66, 150
Elektra 77, 79
Elofsson, Jörgen 121
EMI 10, 33, 63, 66, 69, 71, 78,
    80–1, 109, 128, 132, 139
eMusic 103–5

Enders Analysis 150
England, R. W. 36
Engström, A. 47, 48
European Union Copyright
    Directive (EUCD), 20, 155
Evans, P. 35
evolutionary economics 37–8

Facebook 8, 160, 176
fans 1–2, 7, 10–11, 22, 33, 51, 61,
    87, 92–3, 106, 109, 129, 138,
    144, 147–8, 157–8, 162–3,
    165, 167–8, 176–8
feels-like-free 106
Feist, Leslie 95
Ferguson, D. A. 16–17
file-sharing 2, 4, 64, 66, 150–3,
    156, 167
Fisher, F. 51
Fiss, P. C. 41–2
Florida, R. 16
Forbes 131
Forrester Research 150
Foster, J. 37
Franz Ferdinand 95
Freedman, D. 153
freemium 175
Frith, S. 29

Gelatt, R. 61
geography 15, 124–5
Gerstner, L. V. 116
Ghemawat, P. 35
Gibbons, F. 139
Gilmore, J. H. 15
Girard, A. 13–14
Glassman, R. B. 51
Good Charlotte 95
Goodman, F. 4, 101
Google 7
Gorillaz, The 136
Graceland 132

Graff, G. 95
Grey Album 157
Gronow, P. 61, 88

Hadenius, S. 16–17
Hallencreutz, D. 15, 47–8, 125
Hamel, G. 35
Hamilton, D. B. 37
Hansson, N. 135
Hartley, J. 14–16, 23
Harvey, E. 73, 122
Hax, A.C. 32, 102
Hesmondhalgh, D. 13–14, 17, 20,
    23–5, 31, 49
High School Musical 133
Hirsch, P.M. 13, 20, 22–3, 41–2,
    50, 53–6
Hit Factory, The 123
Hollifield, C. A. 89
Horkheimer, M. 12–13, 28
Horowitz, B. 7
Hoskins, C. 21, 23, 25, 34
Howkins, J. 16
Hu, Y. 90

IFPI 9, 17, 24, 65, 69–72, 75, 78,
    80, 101, 112, 151–3
iMeem 8, 87
Imfeld, C. J. 153
Imogen Heap 176–7
independent (music), 28, 30,
    65–8, 129–30
    label 129–30
    semi-, 30
Ingenious Media 139
Interscope 1, 73, 136
Ipsos-Reid 150

Jackson, Michael 82
Jay-Z 92, 121, 139, 157
Jenkins, H. 53, 89, 147, 157
JYP Entertainment 114

Kaldor, N. 36
Kapferer, J.-N. 130
Karlsson, D. 25–6
Katz, M. 89
Kealy, E. 44
Kelly, K. 135
Kinney 68, 79
Knight, J. A. 25, 27
Konichiwa Records 144–5
Korte, E. 95
Kusek, D. 6

Lala 4, 8, 87
last.fm 8
Lave, J. 39
Lekvall, L. 25–6
Lennon, John 80, 82, 132
Leonard, G. 3, 6, 82
Levine, R. 44
Levinthal, D. A. 36
Leyshon, A. 15, 49–51
licensing 10, 46, 58, 63, 85–6,
    92–101, 108, 132, 139, 141–3,
    168
Liebowitz, S. 151
LimeWire 4, 8
LinkedIn 160
Lister, M. 89
live music 10, 46–7, 49, 53,
    57–61, 71–2, 83, 85, 93, 118,
    136–8, 140, 143, 146, 166
Live Nation 10, 60, 71, 83,
    138–40, 145
lock-in 32, 102
Long Tail, The 90
Lorenz, H.-W. 37

Madonna 77–8, 83, 139, 144, 145
Magnatune 110
major (music company), 28, 33,
    65–71, 101, 103, 113, 129, 144
    definition 28

March, J. G. 1–2, 27, 37, 51, 128,
    140
Marley, Bob 132
Martin, George 120
mash-up 157
Max Martin 121, 144
MCA 74
McFadyen, S. 21, 23, 25, 34
MelOn 104, 114–5
Mercury 63, 73–4
Mermigas, D. 116
Metcalfe, J. S. 3, 37
Meyer, A. D. 38, 51
Meyer, J. 38, 51
Microsoft 4, 95, 163
Miège, B. 13
Miles, R. E. 38–9, 45, 80, 82,
    116
Millard, E. 153
Mitchell, G. 30, 82
Monkees, The 126
Motown 73–4, 133
MP3, 2, 66, 149, 166
MTV 96–7, 126
music producer 40, 119–22, 124,
    126
music publishing 10, 24, 57–8,
    62, 73, 77, 80
Music United 153
music video 65, 101, 122, 126–7,
    147, 158, 160, 167
MusicStation 104
Myrdal, G. 37
MySpace 8, 87, 160, 166

Napster 2, 8, 105, 149
Negus, K. 13, 17, 22–3, 28–30, 42,
    47, 155
Nelson, R. 30, 36–7, 82
Neuman, W .R. 24
Nickelback 77, 140
Nilsson, T. 25

Nine Inch Nails 1, 7, 145, 158–9, 163–4, 176
  Ghosts 1, 2, 111
  Reznor, Trent 1, 92, 111, 145, 163–4, 176–7
  Year Zero 163
Nokia 113, 161
Northern Songs 82

Oberholzer, F. 151
OECD 9, 17
Olin-Scheller, C. 7
Olsen, J. P. 51
Omnifone 104
on-demand 66, 107–8, 115
online piracy 64, 150–2
option value 10, 21, 88, 90, 106, 111, 113, 165
Oram, A. 149
organizational
  adaptation 38, 45
  learning 36–7
Orwall, B. 30
Ouchi, Wi. 51
Ovi 113

Pandora 8, 106
participatory culture 147–8
peer-to-peer 2, 64, 66, 89, 92, 101, 148–51, 153–4, 156, 161
Perrow, C. 51
Peterson, R. A. 41–5
Philips 66
Picard, R. G. 16, 17, 23–7, 32, 34, 71, 89
Pine, B. J. 15
Pisano, G. 36
Planet Earth 138
plunderphonics 157
Poe, R. 62
Polydor 74

Pop Idol 133–5
  American Idol 135
Porter, M. E. 32–3, 35–6, 77, 125
Power, D. 15, 125
Prahalad, C. K. 35
preselection system 22–3, 53, 55
Presley, Elvis 67, 73, 75, 132, 151
pricing 102–3, 109–10, 174
Prince 30, 138
production of culture 29, 42, 44
Pussycat Dolls 95, 136

Qtrax 8
Qualen, J. 61
Queen 80, 126

Radio City Music Hall 92
Radiohead 78, 80, 109, 145
Radzicki, M. J. 37
RCA 63, 66–7, 75–6, 144
Read, O. 61
RealNetworks 104
Reca, A. A. 23
recording studio 2, 119, 122–4
Rhapsody 8, 66, 104–5
RIAA 153
rights holder 21, 89, 98, 104–5, 107–10, 115, 148–50, 152, 156, 167–70, 174–6
Rolling Stones 78, 80, 83
Rosen, C. 30
Rowan, B. 51
Roxette 161–2, 164
royalties 57, 63, 82, 97–9, 104, 132–3, 141–2, 174–5
  mechanical 93
  synchronization 93

Sanctuary Records 74, 139
Saunio, I. 61
Schnur, S. 95
Schön, D. 36–7

Schumpeter, J. 37
Scott, A. J. 49
Senge, P. 37
Seoul Records 114
Shakira 75, 140
Shakur, Tupac 132
Shapiro, C. 21, 24, 32, 34, 102
Shuen, A. 36
Shulman, L. 35
Simon, H. A. 22, 36–7, 51, 89
SK Telecom 114–15
Slash 158
Snow, C. C. 38–9, 45, 73, 116
Sony 10, 63, 66, 71, 75–7, 82, 95,
    113, 134
  Sony BMG 75–6
  Sony Ericsson 113
  Sony Music 10, 63, 71, 75–7,
    134
  Sony/ATV 10, 71, 82
Spears, Britney 121, 158, 168
SpiralFrog 8
Spotify 4, 8, 107, 175
Stalk, G. 35
Star Trek 158
Statute of Anne 18
Sterman, J. D. 35, 37
streaming 107, 115
Strumpf, K. 151
superstar 59, 95, 121, 131–2, 165

Talomma, Tom 121
Tapscott, D. 156
Teece, D. J. 36
Thompson, H. S. 155
Thorburn, D. 53, 89
Thorselius, R. 162
Throsby, D. 13
Timbaland 121
Timberlake, Justin 75, 111, 158
Time 77
Time Warner 77

Tin Pan Alley 62, 100
Tip Jar model 110
Towse, R. 13
Toynbee, J. 118
Tremlett, G. 140

U2, 33, 73, 83, 112, 140
Universal 1, 10, 71–4, 102–3, 133
upstreaming 68, 130
user-generated content 10, 157–9,
    164, 177

value-based pricing 110
Varian, H. R. 21, 24–5, 32, 34,
    37, 102
versioning 111
Victor 18, 62–3, 66, 75–6
Victrola 66
videogames 17, 24, 41, 57, 85–6,
    95–6, 115, 132–3, 147, 164
viral 160, 162, 164
Virgin Records 80–1
Vivendi 69, 72–3
Vogel, H. L. 24, 57

Wallis, R. 58, 99, 129
Warner 10, 30, 68–71, 77–9,
    139
Watts, D. J. 5
WEA 79
Web 2.0, 3
Weibull, L. 16, 17
Weick, K. 51
Welch, W. L. 61
Wenger, E. 39–40
Werde, B. 44
Wernerfelt, B. 35
Westlife 121
Wikström, P. 7, 71, 86, 151
Wilde, D. L. 32, 102
Wildman, S. S. 34
Williams, A. 82, 156

Williams, Pharrell 80, 121
Williams, R. 139
Winehouse, Amy 73, 133
Winter, S. 36–7
WIPO 17, 155–6
Witt, U. 37
Wolf, M. J. 24
word-of-mouth 161

Yahoo!, 7
Yeaman, N. 145
Young, Will 135
YouTube 1, 2, 4, 87, 92, 157–60,
    162–3, 176

Zaid, G. 24
Zanyar, Darin 135